Secrets of Men

Helping You Achieve Your Sexual Best

by

Nicholas A. Natale, Ph.D.

WWW.OAKLEAPRESS.COM

Secrets of Men: Helping You Achieve Your Sexual Best © 2023 by Nicholas A. Natale, Ph.D.. All rights reserved. No part of this book may be used or reproduced in any manner whatsoever without written permission except in the case of brief quotations embodied in critical articles and reviews. For information visit:

www.oakleapress.com

Table of Contents

Foreword 5

Introduction 7

Chapter One: Life Is Full of Secrets 11

Chapter Two: Embrace Your Erotic Profile .... 30.

Chapter Three: Your Sexual Best Is Built 46

Chapter Four: Confidence Is Sexy 66

Chapter Five: Face Sexual Shame 88

Chapter Six: Porn Conditions You 99

Chapter Seven: Own Your Masculinity 118

Chapter Eight: Evoke your Primal Sexual Energy 132

About the Author 142

Addendum: Hyponotic Scripts 143

*The greatest secrets are always hidden
in the most unlikely places.*

— Roald Dahl

Foreword

I am so happy that Dr. Nic has written this book. As a mother of two sons, it is wonderful to see something so compassionately written, real and connection-focused on the topic of sex. The insights and exercises within will be a wonderful resource for practitioners and clients alike.

In a world where most young men get the majority of their sex education from a combination of social media and pornography, often leading to disastrous experiences, unrealistic expectations and sexual dysfunction. Secrets of Men is a compassionate, educational, and practical book that will provide men and the people that love them the insight and resources they need to understand and connect to themselves and others without anxiety or shame.

Essential reading for all men who wish to have meaningful and satisfying sexual experiences.

Kaz Riley,
Sex Educator, Hypnotist and
author of the bestselling book, *Woman*

*The secret of change is to focus all your energy,
not on fighting the old, but on building the new*

— Socrates

Introduction

Welcome to *Secrets of Men: How to Achieve Your Sexual Best*. I suppose that it is inevitable that every practitioner of the healing arts would want to express his or her thoughts in written form. This is my personal contribution. After twenty-three years of practice as a licensed counselor, therapist, doctoral work, certified sex therapist, and hypnotherapist, I wanted to provide a resource for men that would help them explore the art of healthy sex and relationships. In this book, you and I will delve into the deepest and most intimate recesses of the male psyche to uncover secrets and desires often hidden from public view. Through personal stories, expert insights, exercises, and analyses of research by leading experts in the field, my goal is to inspire you to embrace your sexuality and to understand the complexity of your sexual desires.

For too long, men have been expected to conform to rigid societal norms and to suppress their thoughts, fantasies, and desires about sex. This has led to a culture of shame and secrecy surrounding sexual issues with the result that many men feel too ashamed or embarrassed to explore their sexuality. I believe, however, that sex is a natural and essential aspect of the human experience, and that by understanding and embracing our desires, we can lead more fulfilling and satisfying lives.

Through the pages of this book, I share stories of men who have overcome shame and societal expectations by exploring and discovering their true sexual selves. I also provide practical advice for those who may be struggling with sexual issues. My goal is to help them to navigate the often-complex world of male sexuality and help them achieve their sexual best.

Each chapter is designed to be stand-alone. Therefore, feel free to jump to a chapter that appears at this time to be most relevant for you. I encourage you, however, to read chapters you may initially have skipped as your journey with me continues. I hope this book initially will be viewed as a conversation between you and me about how to achieve your sexual best, and in the long run, that it will serve as a resource you can return to time and again.

This book will also give you access to hypnotic sessions intended for your use in achieving your best sexual self. As a hypnotherapist, I have guided a number of men and women in trance as they explore their sexual selves. Many have found it extraordinarily helpful to explore these issues without their critical mental faculties getting in the way.

Hypnosis is a therapeutic tool that can be used to help men explore and understand what may be hidden in the recesses of their psyches concerning sex. By inducing a state of deep relaxation and heightened suggestibility, hypnosis can allow them to access the deep parts of their minds in order to explore their desires and fantasies in a safe and supportive environment.

During a hypnosis session, a trained practitioner can guide you through a series of suggestions and visualizations to help you overcome inhibitions or anxieties that may be preventing you from fully embracing your sexuality. In this way, access to the subconscious mind through hypnosis can help you uncover hidden desires, release unproductive beliefs that may be inhibiting you, and explore latent aspects of your sexual identity.

Hypnosis can also be used to help men overcome sexual dysfunction in order to improve their sexual performance. By addressing underlying psychological issues such as anxiety or self-doubt, hypnosis can help men overcome performance anxiety and achieve a more satisfying and fulfilling sexual experience.

Suffice it to say, hypnosis can be a powerful tool for men seeking to explore and understand their sexuality. By accessing the deeper parts of their psyches, hypnosis can help men overcome inhibitions and anxieties in a safe and supportive environment in order to embrace and eventually to fulfill their true sexual desires. You will find the text of hypnotic scripts in the addendum as well hypnotic recordings you will be able to access for your personal use via the Internet.

I fully acknowledge that the stories and illustrations throughout *Secrets of Men* are written from a heterosexual male perspective. However, the insights, exercises, and encouragement within are intended for every man and masculine-self as they explore their own sexual and relationship journey. My therapeutic and coaching practice encompasses individuals who identify as men, women, and non-binary genders in traditional and non-traditional relationship structures.

Whether you are a man seeking to understand your own desires, or someone interested in gaining a deeper understanding of the male psyche, Secrets of Men offers a compassionate and inspiring look at how to achieve your sexual best. I hope this book will inspire you to embrace your own sexuality and to live a more fulfilling and authentic life.

Chapter One: Life Is Full of Secrets

H. P. Lovecraft [1890-1937], an American writer of fantasy and horror fiction, began one of his famous stories with these two sentences: "The most merciful thing in the world, I think, is the inability of the human mind to correlate all its contents. We live on a placid island of ignorance in the midst of black seas of infinity, and it was not meant that we should voyage far."

I believe Lovecraft was right about one thing when he referred to, "a placid island of ignorance in the midst of black seas of infinity." Life is full of secrets, and perhaps it's true we are not meant to know all of them. Nevertheless, I have found that most men and women harbor hidden secrets that form their beliefs about sex and that it can be important and productive for them to delve deeply inside themselves to discover what they are. Those beliefs can then be examined, and if any are not serving the person well, banished and replaced with something new and true. This can be extremely gratifying, but even more important, it can result in the individual being able to achieve a better and more satisfying sex life.

I personally find secrets to be fascinating. I love everything about them: secret societies, secret knowledge, secret rendezvous, secret missions. Secrets are fascinating because they indicate that we do not know everything we could know; that there is more out there. Secrets are like pieces of a puzzle. Often when a piece falls into place, what has been hidden comes to light, and we finally see the full picture. What someone learns in that moment can change his life forever—often in a very positive way.

Uncovering secrets is something of a hobby of mine, and it's one reason why, as a therapist, I strive to dig deeply into the human psyche. Helping individuals understand and unlock their personal strengths, helping them come to know themselves at a deep level and work through difficult aspects of their lives can be amazing and extraordinarily rewarding.

In therapy, the word "catharsis" refers to an insight or revelation that leads to a purifying emotional release—a unique "aha" moment that may unlock and release years of conflicting emotional patterns. I have witnessed this happen many times and can assure you that when it does it is nothing less than a life-changing moment for my clients.

I love discovering how things work. As a naturally curious person, I am particularly curious about sex in relationships. If I were a betting man, which I am, I would wager that you're reading this book because, like me, you are curious about sex and relationships as well.

The intent of this book is to introduce you to seven key sexual secrets that will enable you to unlock your best sexual self. It's true. Secrets are out there that can make a significant difference in your life. Those who know the secrets are already capable and confident lovers, and you can become one of them. This book, *Secrets of Men*, will reveal those secrets so that you can achieve your sexual and relationship best.

Who Is This Book Written For?

It's important for readers to understand that this book is not meant for fake-alpha males whatabes. You know the type, guys who try to become "top dog" in every room they're in, sizing everyone up, and limiting relationships with women to just get what they want from them. Nor is it for those looking for the next craze in the "PUA" (Pick Up Artists) scene. The guys who frequent bars and clubs in order to meet women and convince them to go home with them for a one-night stand. This book is not written for someone who is simply looking for a quick fix to his sad and broken attraction game.

Secrets of Men is for the guy who wants to form a sincere relationship with someone and delve deeply into that relationship by mastering his full sexual potential. In other words, it is intended for the man who wants a mutually fulfilling sexual relationship with a woman. This book is intended to help him adopt the right mindset and provide insights and information concerning sexual practices that will help him accomplish his desire to form and perpetuate a healthy, striving and mutually fulfilling sexual relationship with his wife, partner, or girlfriend.

Sexual Issues

At this point, we need to pause and make sure you're doing okay. If you are experiencing erectile dysfunction or other identified sexual issue, the first step is to have a talk with your family doctor or your urologist. A number of factors can lead to ED, Premature Ejaculation, Lack of Desire, and other sexual issues. Your sexual function is susceptible to age, medical, trauma, and other factors. You will want to ensure that the sexual issue you are experiencing is being treated effectively. Once any medical or physiological contributors have been ruled out, you're ready for the insights explored below. Every client I work with is seen by a medical professional for an evaluation before moving into the process that follows.

It's Story Time: Paul and Tonya

A common situation I come across in my clinical work is that of Paul and Tonya. Paul and Tonya are in their early thirties. Both are successful and involved in their community with a number of friends. Overall, they are happy in their relationship. When they first met, the sexual chemistry between them was intense. Unfortunately, now that a few years have passed, their mutual attraction is not what it once was. Their once intense sexual chemistry has faded into what I call a "dead bedroom." Sex for Paul and Tonya has become routine, boring, and unsatisfying. When they first came to me, the chemistry just wasn't there anymore. They both knew it was happening, but they couldn't find a way to reverse the decline. One of the problems had to do with familiarity. Spending too much time together resulted in a lack of mystery and sexual tension between them. That "special feeling" that once existed was nowhere to be found. The bottom line was that they no longer put much effort into their sexual relationship. Their emotional connection waned, and they no longer communicated as they once did. It was clear that something needed to be done to turn the situation around before their marriage ended up on the rocks.

Paul was concerned, and no wonder. He instinctively understood where this could lead. He was fully aware their relationship had gone off track, but he didn't know why it had or how to fix it. He thought the problem must have been his—that he must not have been doing something right.

Like most men, Paul is a "fixer," and so he took this trait into the bedroom and did his best to remedy the situation—but try as he might, nothing seemed to work. Men, Paul included, tend to be more risk-takers than women. But Paul was not able to get Tonya to move beyond what the two of them had become accustomed to, and so the downhill spiral continued with an increasingly negative effect on Paul's confidence and performance. He had slipped into a performance mindset and was not connecting with Tonya on an emotional level because of it.

By focusing on performance rather than his pleasure and Tonya's, he had become too caught up in his own head. What he was trying to do to fix the situation became the very things that ended up sabotaging their time together. It's a common trap. When a guy begins to worry that a situation is going wrong, it affects his performance. His worrying ensures that it becomes self-fulfilling—his fear becomes his reality. Such concerns can pull a man out of his body and into his head, and one thing we know to be true is this: "Where the mind goes the body follows."

For Paul, the result of his worrying led him to a place where he was unable to form a full erection, or any erection at all, and this resulted in more and more frustration. Obviously, it had the effect of shutting things down between them; resulting in more dissatisfaction.

Suffice to say the "fix it mentality" inevitably leads to a downward spiral. It starts with poor performance, followed by a lack of connection, followed by dissatisfying sexual encounters, which lead to fewer sexual encounters overall, and finally, to the lack of an emotional connection with a partner. It is a very common dynamic in couples who are struggling.

It is a fact that the vast majority of men who visit their family doctor or urologist for suspected erectile dysfunction [ED] do not have a physiological problem at all. The "plumbing" is working fine. This can also be true for someone unable to reach climax during intercourse. The problem these men face is psychological in nature. Men with ADHD are even more likely than others to suffer from such issues. Their minds may be racing, jumping around to so many different things going on in their heads that they are unable to remain in their bodies long enough to enjoy the physical sensations of sex.

The majority of men who come into my office have reached similar situations. They usually do not want to talk to another man about their inability to perform sexually, but like Paul, without realizing it, they have dug themselves into a deep hole because of their "performance mentality." They no longer connect emotionally with their partners. This likely happened because they have stopped seeking pleasure. Instead, they are striving to perform. The result is the dead bedroom. Neither Paul nor Tonya can feel fulfilled when in a performance mindset.

Fortunately, for those in a situation that resembles what Paul was going through, help is available. This book will reveal secrets Paul used to expand his sexual experience to the point where he was able to fully satisfy both himself and Tonya. This included how to talk about and communicate his sexual needs and desires, which is of utmost importance. It's a fact that many men shy away from expressing or even acknowledging their thoughts about sex, often because they've been conditioned to think sex is dirty, or even feel shame that they even have certain kinds of sexual desires. The same is often true for women, which quite naturally exacerbates the problem. Perhaps, for example, a man's wife or partner has been conditioned to believe that sex is wrong. He may bring up something about their sexual relationship in an attempt to improve it, and because of her conditioning she may say, "Why do you think about sex so much?" This will, of course, serve to reinforce his tendency toward reticence and cut short the chance for improvement.

Sexual Fulfillment Is Fun and Bonding

The truth is that sex is a basic human need. A situation such as Paul and Tonya's is not only devastating, it is tragic because the sex between them was something they both really enjoyed early in their relationship. Sex in a relationship is one of the most fun and emotionally fulfilling aspects of life. It's true. The sexual experience in a relationship is emotionally bonding. Like it or not, just about every human being has sexual desires, and there's absolutely no reason to be embarrassed about it.

So let me ask you: "Is your sexual experience fulfilling? Is it fun? Is it emotionally bonding for your relationship?"

A Cultural Perspective

For centuries, societal expectations have imposed a set of rigid norms on men that have dictated how they should behave, feel, and think about sex. These expectations are largely a product of historical traditional gender roles and cultural beliefs that have been passed down through generations. In addition, recent cultural pressures have called into question qualities of masculinity. As a result, many men have felt pressured to suppress their thoughts, fantasies, and desires related to sex in order to conform to these societal norms. This has given rise to a culture of shame and secrecy surrounding men's sexual issues, ultimately limiting their ability to explore and embrace their sexuality.

Traditional gender roles: The influence of traditional gender roles has played a significant role in shaping men's attitudes and behaviors towards sex both for the positive as well as the negative. Men are often expected to maintain a strong, stoic demeanor and be the dominant partner in sexual relationships. This has led to a lot of men focusing so much on their partner's desires and less on their own expressed wants and desires. This can encourage men to be emotionally detached and to suppress their desires and fantasies related to sex.

Stereotypes and expectations: Men have been subjected to various stereotypes and expectations regarding their sexual prowess and performance. Society often expects men to be sexually experienced, always ready for sex, and able to satisfy their partners. These expectations create immense pressure on men, which may lead to anxiety, low self-esteem, and a fear of failure in sexual situations.

Shame and secrecy: The culture of shame and secrecy surrounding men's sexual issues has made it difficult for them to openly discuss their thoughts, fantasies, and desires. Men are often afraid of being judged, ridiculed, or stigmatized for expressing their sexual needs and desires. This lack of open communication and understanding may lead to unhealthy and unfulfilling sexual relationships.

Insufficient Sex Education: Comprehensive sexual education that addresses the diverse needs and experiences of both men and women is crucial to fostering healthy attitudes towards sex. However, many educational systems and societal norms have historically focused on reproductive aspects and prevention of sexually transmitted infections, neglecting the importance of communication, consent, and exploration of one's sexuality. This lack of education and resources contributes to men's inability to fully understand and embrace their sexual desires and fantasies.

Mental health implications: The pressure to conform to rigid societal norms and the culture of shame and secrecy surrounding men's sexual issues can have negative consequences on men's mental health. Men may experience anxiety, depression, and low self-esteem as a result of feeling unable to express and explore their sexuality fully.

To break the cycle of shame and secrecy surrounding men's sexual issues, it is essential for a man to challenge and redefine his mindset surrounding sexuality. Open communication must be encouraged, as well as the promotion of effective sexual education, and the fostering of an environment within relationships in which men feel comfortable exploring their sexuality with regard to their masculinity and desires without the fear of judgment or stigma.

Porn and Hook-Up Culture

Consider, for example, a young man who grew up in a home where not much affection was displayed between mom and dad. Let's say that this young man discovers porn online, and now watches it on a regular basis. Do you suppose his porn use will have an effect when he is with an actual sexual partner? Will he bring what he learned on PornHub to his sexual encounters? I think we can all agree that it is fairly reasonable to think that his porn use will have some effect on his thoughts, emotions, and actions during sex.

Men can be conditioned by porn. We will go into more detail later, but for now, you need to recognize the central truth that regular porn use has an effect on a person's sexual experience. It is not uncommon for men who have been conditioned by porn to tell me that their partners are not responding as they should. These men think they are supposed to perform like the male actors in those videos, and that their partners should perform the same way as the female actors. It is not uncommon for these guys to be in their thirties, and yet they still think that's how a sexual encounter should go. What they do not understand is that the pornographic videos they watch are pure fantasy. More than likely, they have been highly edited; the boring stuff has been cut out. Moreover, she's not really having one orgasm after another—it's all an act. In addition, scenes have probably been moved around, perhaps brought in from action shot at a different time. The companies who produce these videos want to keep viewers interested—they want them glued to the screen. That's how they make a living. Unfortunately, it can have a devastating effect on a guy's sexual experience.

Porn isn't the only thing that can lead to ideas about sex that can be counterproductive to the health of a long-term relationship. We are living in a hook-up culture. The mentality that being a member of the hook-up culture typically creates can have a profoundly negative effect on a person's ability to connect emotionally with a sexual partner. Sex with a hook-up partner can be very different from sex with a loved one.

Those heavily influenced by porn and the hook-up culture typically have or will develop an unsatisfying sexual relationship with a permanent partner. Peggy Orenstein, author of *Boys & Sex: Young Men on Hookups, Porn, Consent and Navigating the New Masculinity* (Harper, 2020) has said that her research indicates girls are disconnected from their bodies and desires, and that disconnect radiates outward to negatively affect their intimate relationships. Young men and boys, on the other hand, are disconnected from their hearts, and that not only affects them in a negative way personally, it radiates outward and affects their intimate relationships in negative ways as well. No wonder a mindset change must take place before they can fully realize sexual fulfillment in a long-term relationship. The mechanics of the sex act in porn and in hook-ups is likely the only thing that's similar to sex in a permanent relationship. Nothing else is the same.

Secrets of Men will explain that an important way to achieve the best sex and to find fulfillment in your relationship is by forming and maintaining a close connection or bond with one's partner. Many of the secrets to be revealed will challenge readers' mindsets so that they are able to transform themselves in ways that make it possible for them to connect with their partners on a deep emotional level.

In summary, the expectations of men who have been conditioned by porn and the hook-up culture are often totally unrealistic. This can result in dissatisfaction, guilt, and fear because they think they are not performing adequately.

My Story

I knew that sex was important to me from an early age. Beginning in elementary school, I was already aware of my body and sexual interest. However, like most families of my generation, sex was not talked about at home, though physical displays of affection were always given to me and my sister by our parents. The majority of my childhood was spent playing in safety, with plenty of room to explore the acres of woods in my backyard. Like so many boys of my generation, the day came when I found my father's stash of *Playboy* and *Penthouse* magazines. They'd been carefully hidden away, and obviously were meant to stay that way. Jackpot!

I enjoyed stealing away and spending time with those magazines. However, I also became very aware of the feelings of guilt and shame that came with it. When I think back to those times, I can clearly see how the connection between sex and shame and guilt coalesced together to form my general approach to sex. It became difficult to separate one from another. For years later, whenever I became aroused the infamous shame and guilt wasn't far behind. Though I loved sex as a teen and as a man, guilt and shame were always present as well. Sex became miserable. The toxic trifecta persisted for years.

The internal conflict soared to new heights when I became more involved in the small Southern Baptist Church near my home. I was taught that sex was a particular kind of evil reserved for the worst of earthly negative consequences and eternal damnation. To a young man surging with sexual appetite, and yet one who wanted so desperately to quiet the internal struggle with shame and guilt, I searched desperately for some form of reprieve that would also honor my faith. Throughout my high school years, my desires got the best of me, as did my guilt, which overwhelmed me to the point that I confessed to my pastor that I had been with my girlfriend.

What an embarrassing experience that was! His manner was kind and loving, but the words he spoke filled me with even more shame and guilt. He told me such actions were going to ruin me as a person and ruin my future. He made it clear that the best step for me was to get married instead of "burning with passion."

The solution? Marriage!

So that is what I did. I got married as soon as I could—at the age of 20 while still in college. It was with someone I cared about, of course, but to be perfectly honest, what drove me was my desire for sex. I thought marriage would take away this deep internal conflict once and for all. That's what I had been taught. Sex in marriage was going to be something wonderful and beautiful—but that's not how it worked out. What transpired was a long period of unfulfilling experiences. Instead of living in the state of bliss I believed I'd been promised, I was trapped.

The Fundamental Truth about Sex

The foundational truth is that it's okay to experience your full sexual self. There is absolutely nothing wrong with it. As a result of what I went through, I know that it takes a lot of effort to work to overcome negative conditioning that has come about as the result of being taught that sex is wrong and that enjoying it is shameful. What I know to be true is that sex is one of the most important and wonderful experiences of our existence. When it is expressed in a healthy relationship, the individuals are more satisfied, emotionally connected and grounded.

What Are Your Sex Scripts?

As we uncover the first secret in Chapter Two, you will be given information and exercises that will help you determine the ideas and attitudes that you absorbed about sex growing up and in the culture in which we live. This will help you learn a great deal about the script you are operating from. Once you see it, you will be in a better position to start making changes. Your transformation will begin. But be prepared. It will not be easy. It's going to take some effort on your part.

I say this because I have found that not every client is ready to start the transformation process. I believe that most of us of the male persuasion like to think of ourselves as men rather than boys, but I have found that, unfortunately, some are stuck in what might be called "the Peter Pan syndrome," "perpetual childhood," or "immature personality disorder" (there's no such diagnosis in the DSM). In other words, they do not seem to want to grow up.

For example, I once counseled a college student, a musician, who told me that his girlfriend wanted sex more often, but that he kept putting her off. One reason was that he was a classical guitarist getting ready for an upcoming concert. That's understandable. No worries.

Nevertheless, he kept bringing this up in our sessions that they weren't having sex, and so I finally asked him to tell me more about it, "What's going on here?"

He said, "I don't know. She wants to have sex more often. She's trying but I keep turning her down."

I said, "Okay, but why is that a problem? Every couple must find their own rhythm in how often they're together. Perhaps you just want sex less."

"No! That's not it. I want sex more often too... Well, to tell the truth, it's the condoms."

I said, "Oh, I see. You don't like the feel of condoms."

"No, no, that's not it. I don't mind wearing them. It's just that condoms are too expensive."

I paused for a moment with a blank stare and then said, "What kind of condoms are you using? I didn't think inflation hit that hard."

We both laughed. Then he continued, "You see, I'm saving up for a new video game."

After another blank stare, I said, "So you're telling me that you would rather save for a $65 game than spend five dollars for 15 sexual encounters with your girlfriend?" (Yeah, I know, I dug at him a little bit.)

"Well, yeah," he said. "PlayStation is better. I just gotta save up for this game I want."

This was not the first time I'd heard something like that, although some men say something a bit more subtle, such as, "Porn is easier than being with a girlfriend." There are so many ways the same sentiment is being expressed today. Perhaps you have come across something similar in your friend group.

Secrets of Men

The Ability to Change Is a Sign of Maturity

The ability to change your mind about something is one of the most powerful aspects of maturation, and it seems to be beyond the ability of some. As it turned out, that ability is what enabled Paul to turn around the dead bedroom that he and Tonya were experiencing. I was able to provide Paul with an honest, open, and safe place to explore and identify the root causes of his and Tonya's unfulfilling sexual relationship. Before long, we discovered what was behind it—the major problem being his belief that he needed to control his sexual performance. This filled him with anxiety and tension—quite literally, it shut him down and prevented him from being able to experience sexual pleasure. You might say he had unintentionally placed his performance mindset between himself and Tonya.

It took some time, and it took some coaching, but once Paul was able to get back into his body and fully experience touch again, he was able to build new skills. Armed with those skills and trusting the process, his body responded as we hoped and thought it would, and he and Tonya became true partners.

Something we've learned since the research by Masters & Johnson was conducted in the 1960s is that when we get out of our heads and allow ourselves to be present in our bodies, the body almost always performs flawlessly. This was true for Paul. By focusing on being present and experiencing the pleasure of the touch he was giving and receiving, his psychological block disappeared, and his body reacted in the way he'd always wanted. What came as a result was his liberating, cathartic, "Aha!" moment, and it was clear sailing for Paul and Tonya from that day forward.

Do You Have What It Takes To Change?

You're about to take a journey that will challenge what you once thought was true. In fact, you may discover that you have built your whole sex life on myths and illusions that are quite simply false. Now is the time to learn the truth, to unlock the secrets in order to achieve more, to achieve your sexual best. It is time to be challenged by the *Secrets of Men*. The insights, stories, and opportunities you are about to discover are derived from leading research, my 20+ years of clinical experience, cultural trends, and spiritual perspectives.

I'm going to ask you to consider two intentions before you proceed into the chapters of this book that follow: Mastery and Mindset.

First, in Jack Donovan's book, *The Way of Men,* he identifies five characteristics that he believes define traditional masculinity. As controversial as his ideas may be, I believe that Donovan was correct to include mastery as one of the characteristics. Mastery of a craft or skill is seen as a demonstration of competence, confidence, and self-reliance. I want you to be aware that your ability to achieve mastery of your sexual self is something that will lead you to embody and thereby exude competence and confidence. To help you achieve this, I am going to ask you to complete a number of "Intentional Opportunities" as we go forward and will invite you to take the time to do the exercises indicated. They can make all the difference in your sexual and relational experiences.

Second, it's imperative to be able to shift your mindset based on new information so that it will be possible for you to operate in a new and different way. That ability to change your mindset will not only help you in the bedroom, it will help in many other aspects of your life. If you have that ability or are willing to put forth the effort to achieve it, you have come to the right place. In the next chapter you will begin to learn seven secrets that can actually change your life and your experience in the bedroom so that you will be able to achieve your sexual best.

And that, my friend, can be a giant step toward creating a life that's well worth living.

Chapter Two: Embrace Your Erotic Profile

The first secret we will explore centers on knowing yourself sexually.

Over the years I have found that the most effective process for discovering your sexual self is to identify your Erotic Profile—it's a crucial aspect of personal growth and self-discovery. Understanding your own desires, boundaries, and preferences can help you navigate intimate relationships with more confidence as well as attain a higher level of satisfaction. Sexual self-awareness also makes it possible for you to communicate effectively with you partner, which almost certainly will lead to a more fulfilling and enjoyable sexual experiences. By exploring and embracing your own sexuality, you can enhance your overall sense of well-being and improve your relationships with others. With that in mind, the first secret is:

Embrace Your Erotic Profile

Sex is more than something that you do. It's more than behavior, biochemistry, or some unseen primal energy. You have a sexual self that grows, changes, evolves, that can provide a lifetime of deep connections. You have your own unique erotic profile. Getting to know your profile and embracing it is an important part of building a loving and exciting environment for you and your partner to share. More importantly, it will empower you with the confidence to be able to express and explore your best sexual self.

Xavier's Journey

Xavier came to see me after experiencing symptoms similar to erectile dysfunction. He had been struggling for nearly two years. "Worry, disappointment, and avoiding," were the three words he used to describe the thoughts he was having about his sexual self.

As our conversation continued, he also added the word, "Failure."

Xavier said, "I'm a failure. I'm a failure to her, and I'm a failure as a man."

How devastating! His words hung heavy in me. It seemed there had to be a lot more to the story—we were just getting started.

I learned he dearly loved and desired his fiancé. In the beginning, things between them had gone well. He didn't have any issues about performing back then, and he felt as though they were both satisfied with the sex life they shared.

However, things changed after he discovered that she kissed another guy while on a girls' trip. It happened with some random dude in a bar and was done as the result of a bet that she lost. When she told Xavier about it, she thought it funny—she thought Xavier might get a kick out of hearing about it.

But he did not.

At first Xavier tried to shrug it off and play it as if it was no big deal. But when he brought it up again in an argument about dinner, they both caught a glimpse of the fact this was a bigger deal than he was letting on.

"I couldn't get it out of my head," he said. "Even at night, I found myself thinking about it. What else did I not know? Why would she think it would be okay? Would it be okay in reverse—if I kissed some random girl?"

As time went by, they had more than one fight about it. In fact, it became a theme for him to bring it up anytime it served him. But that was not the worst part. It also began to affect his ability to perform when they were together.

I asked, "How do you think her kissing another guy shows up during sex?"

"In my head I know it's no big deal. If I'd been there, I'd probably have dogpiled with the rest of the group for her to do it. That's just how we are. No big deal." He paused for a second or two, and then said, "But now it's all I can think about. Now when I try to have sex, it doesn't work. Nothing. I can't get out of my head."

It was clear that Xavier loved his fiancé. I also knew that nothing was physically wrong with his gentiles. I'd asked him to see a urologist just to confirm that, and his exam turned out fine. The urologist suggested that he continue to work with me. What was going on was psychological rather than physical, which is often the case.

As we explored the issue, Xavier began to see the connection between his issue with ED and his own insecurities. In his case, Xavier's insecurities were centered on the discovery that his mother had cheated on his dad several times before his parents got divorced. It became clear that events in the bar were not really the source of the issue—they were the catalyst that triggered it.

With time, Xavier was able to work through his issues; his insecurities were addressed in an effective way. He also learned how to be more present when he was with his fiancé, and it didn't take long for the improvements to completely transform their relationship. Perhaps as a result, I received an invitation to the wedding.

In Daniel Watter's groundbreaking book entitled *The Essential Importance of the Penis,* he stresses the significance of addressing male sexual issues by considering that "the penis is a conduit for a male emotion and thus regulates the closeness/distance that men will allow themselves to experience in intimate relationships." What Xavier experienced seems to have been an example of this. As the center of emotional regulation, a man's penis reflects areas of emotional conflict that may be taking place deep down, below the surface.

When we consider Xavier's case, perhaps it becomes more apparent why it's important to spend time investing in becoming aware of your sexual self. In order to achieve your sexual best, you must be willing and able to look at and see what is taking place inside. Sex is more than behavior—it's more than emotion or passion. Sex is an integrated part of you that's incredibly powerful, life giving, and vital to your overall satisfaction in life.

Sex is Vital

Sexuality is an essential part of our lives, but it can often be a difficult topic to navigate. From social stigmas to personal insecurities, many people find it challenging to embrace their sexual selves. However, knowing your sexual self is crucial for personal growth and happiness, as well as for building healthy and satisfying intimate relationships.

To press this point, below are several key passages from some of the biggest voices in sex and relationships in our culture on the topic of knowing yourself sexually:

> "When we know our own sexual selves, we can be more confident and assertive in our intimate relationships, which can lead to deeper connections and greater sexual satisfaction."
>
> —Ian Kerner, author of
> *She Comes First: The Thinking Man's Guide to Pleasuring a Woman*

> "Understanding your own sexuality is key to your happiness and well-being. It's not just about what you like or don't like, it's about knowing yourself on a deeper level and being able to communicate your needs and desires to your partner."
>
> —Esther Perel, author of
> *Mating in Captivity: Unlocking Erotic Intelligence*

> "Sexual self-knowledge is a powerful tool for self-discovery, self-expression, and personal growth. When we know ourselves intimately, we can make better choices about our relationships and our lives."
>
> —Dossie Easton, author of
> *The Ethical Slut: A Guide to Infinite Sexual Possibilities*

Your Erotic Profile

An Erotic Profile is a description of an individual's sexuality and sexual desires. Forming your Erotic Profile is an empowering experience that can help you know more about yourself and help you communicate who you are and what you desire sexually while with your intimate partner. It explores four key components of sexuality: 1) Your Personal Sexual Script; 2) Your Sexual Interest Panel; 3) Sexual Fantasies; and 4) Journal Entries.

Before you begin, find a journal or notebook where this information can be stored securely and in one location. You might want to use a dedicated paper journal or a single document on your computer or tablet. You're about to explore some extremely intimate and exciting parts of your most vulnerable self, so keep it secret, keep it safe!

You ideally will share your Erotic Profile with your intimate partner at some point. She may even want to take the journey with you from the start and answer the same questions. If that's the case, perhaps a shared paper journal or shared document would work, but it will need to be kept easily accessible to both of you.

Your Personal Sexual Script

The first thing to understand is how attitudes, beliefs, and experiences have shaped your approach to sex. This is a key aspect of knowing your sexual self. Sexual script theory is a social psychological framework that seeks to explain how people learn and enact sexual behaviors and roles within the context of culture and society. It suggests that individuals' sexual behaviors and attitudes are influenced by social norms, expectations, and cultural values.

Knowing your own sexual preferences, desires, and boundaries is essential for building a healthy relationship with yourself. By taking the time to explore your own beliefs, attitudes and desires, you can develop a deeper sense of self-awareness and self-acceptance. This, in turn, can improve your self-confidence and help you feel more comfortable in your own skin.

Furthermore, sexual self-awareness can have a positive impact on your intimate relationships. When you have a clear understanding of your own sexual needs and desires, you will be better equipped to communicate them to your partner. This can help to create more fulfilling sexual experiences for both you and her, and it can help you build trust and intimacy in the relationship. Additionally, understanding your own boundaries and limitations can help you set healthy boundaries in your relationships and avoid uncomfortable or harmful situations.

Sexual self-awareness can also have a positive impact on your overall well-being. Sexual expression can be a powerful tool for reducing stress and anxiety. It can improve your mood and promote relaxation and sleep. By knowing your sexual self and embracing your sexual self, you can tap into these benefits and experience a greater sense of physical and emotional well-being.

Determining your sexual script involves reflecting on your own personal values, attitudes, beliefs, and experiences related to sexuality, as well as considering how social and cultural factors have influenced your sexual behaviors and desires. Below are some questions that can help you explore your sexual script. To begin your sexual script exploration, answer each question below by leaning in to your first, instinctive response. Try not to answer based on someone else's ideal or "shoulds" about sex:

1. What was your first sexual experience like, and how did it shape your views of sexuality?
2. How have your sexual attitudes, interests, and behaviors changed over time, and what influenced those changes?
3. What is your ideal sexual scenario, and how does it differ from your current sexual experiences?
4. What messages about sex and sexuality have you received from your family, religion, culture, or society at large?

5. What are your thoughts on sexual experimentation and trying new things, and how does that fit into your sexual script?
6. How do you define a healthy sexual relationship?
7. What role does gender play in your sexual experiences and desires?
8. What are your thoughts and feelings about casual sex versus committed relationships?
9. What influence has porn played in shaping your sexual experience?
10. What does sex mean to you?

Your Sexual Desire Panel

Sex and desire are complex and multifaceted topics. People can have different sexual desires, which can vary widely in intensity, frequency, and type. A range of factors contributes to the development of sexual desires including biological, psychological, and social factors. Let's explore some of the ways.

Biological factors typically play a significant role. Hormones such as testosterone and estrogen have been linked to sexual arousal and desire. Men usually have higher levels of testosterone than women, which may contribute to their greater sexual desire. Genetics also play a role. For example, some studies have found that genes related to dopamine, a neurotransmitter associated with pleasure and reward, may be associated with greater sexual desire.

Psychological factors such as personality and life experiences can also shape a person's sexual desires. Research suggests that people who are more open to new experiences, and who are less irrational and fearful, tend to have more diverse and adventurous sexual desires.

People can have different sexual desires that are shaped not only by their genetics, personality, and life experiences, but also by their culture and religion. To create a healthy atmosphere for sexual expression, it's important to understand and respect the diversity of sexual desires in order to create a safe and accepting environment in which people are able to explore their sexuality.

Knowing your own sexual desire is important for a number of reasons. Here are a few key reasons why:

Personal fulfillment: Understanding your own sexual desires can help you experience greater personal fulfillment and satisfaction in your sexual experiences. By knowing what you like and want, you can communicate your needs more effectively to your partner, and engage in sexual activities that are enjoyable and fulfilling for you.

Healthy relationships: Being aware of your own sexual desires can help you form healthier relationships with your partners. When you are able to communicate your needs and desires clearly, you are more likely to have a relationship that is built on mutual respect, trust, and understanding.

Sexual health: Understanding your own sexual desires can also help you maintain good sexual health. When you know what you want and need from sexual experiences, you are more likely to engage in safer sex practices, and to make choices that are in line with your values and beliefs.

Personal growth: Finally, exploring your own sexual desires can be a form of personal growth and self-discovery. By understanding and accepting your own sexuality, you can gain a deeper understanding of yourself and your own needs, and become more confident and comfortable with your own sexuality.

Knowing your own sexual desires is an important aspect of overall health and well-being. It can help you form healthy relationships, experience personal fulfillment, and engage in safe and satisfying sexual experiences.

In exercise on the page opposite this one, rate with a Yes!, No! or Maybe, record your answers in your journal. Then talk with your partner about your responses.

Know Your Sexual Desires

Kissing	Kissing in various forms whether engaged in sex or not
Outfits	Willing to wear outfits for your partner
Masturbation	Sexual self-pleasure or with your partner
Scent	Scent or smell of a partner being a factor in sex and arousal
Role Playing	Acting out various roles in a sexual context
Orgasm	The experience of sexual climax
Stripping	Open to stripping or being stripped by your partner
Anal play without sex	Play with anus but no penetration
Porn with partner	Using porn while with a partner, with or without sex
Porn alone	Using porn while by yourself, with our without masturbation
Giving oral sex	Providing oral-genital stimulation to a partner
Receiving oral sex	Receiving oral-genital stimulation from a partner
Fantasy	Creating or remembering sexual images and scenes in imagination
Multiple partners	Engaging in sexual activity with multiple partners simultaneously
Dirty talk	Having sexually explicit talk during sex or as foreplay
Cuddling	Embracing or holding one another, with or without sex
Pictures/video	Taking pictures/video of each other
Sex outside of bedroom	Having sex in locations other than the bedroom
Sensual massage	Giving or receiving sensual or tantric massage
Being watched	Engaging in sexual activity where others could observe
Watching others	Watching others engage in sexual activity
Roleplay	Roleplaying before, during, or after sex
Being in control	Being in charge of when, where, position, during, etc.
Foreplay	Sexual activity preceding intercourse intended to arouse
Music	Listening to music while having sex
Variety	Being open to try new things sexually with your partner
Rough sex	Enjoying rough or raw sex with each other
Sex in public	Engaging in sexual activity in public places, not necessarily watched
Use sex toys	Being free to use sex toys either alone or in sex with partner
Playfulness	Having a sense of humor and being carefree in sexual activity
Anal intercourse	Giving or receiving anal intercourse
Afterplay	Continuing to interact sexually after intercourse
Hairpulling	Pulling or having your hair pulled during sex
Stress relief	Sexual activity as a means of reducing stress
Sexual communication	Being able to talk openly about sex outside of sex
Make up sex	Using sex as a means to make up after an argument/fight
Orgasm denial	Agreeing to allow your partner to deny you an orgasm
Impact play	Spanking, biting, choking during sex
BDSM	Engaging in bondage, dominance, and /or submission
Spiritual Connectedness	Emphasizing spiritually connecting as part of your sex
Fetish	Aroused by a other objects or nonsexual part of the body
Cuckolding	Sexually aroused by your partner having sex with another person
Sexting	Texting suggestively with words, pics, or video

Sexual Fantasies

Sexual fantasies are imaginary situations or scenarios that an individual finds sexually arousing or stimulating. They can involve a wide range of thoughts, feelings, and sensations, and can vary in intensity and content from one person to another.

Some common sexual fantasies include imagining sexual encounters with a particular person or type of person, engaging in taboo or forbidden sexual acts, experiencing sexual dominance or submission, or exploring new sexual experiences or situations. Sexual fantasies can be triggered by a variety of stimuli, such as visual, auditory, or tactile sensations, as well as emotional or psychological states.

It's important to note that sexual fantasies are a normal and healthy part of human sexuality, and many people engage in them regularly, either alone or with a partner. However, it's also important to distinguish between fantasy and reality, and to ensure that all sexual activity is safe and consensual.

For this portion of your Erotic Profile, write down one or two of your sexual fantasies. Where would it take place? Who is there? What are you doing?

Journal Entries

Journal Entries are updates or small discoveries you have made and recorded along your journey. Who you are now is not who you will always be. You may have a sexual interest today that will change, develop and evolve over time. In a healthy sexual individual, such things are constantly evolving and becoming more, and so it's important to recognize that and chronicle it. That's the purpose of this part of your journal. It's where you can record what you have learned about your sexual self. Here are some specific ways that it can be beneficial regarding your sex life:

Emotional regulation: Writing about your emotions can help you identify and label your feelings, which can be helpful in regulating your emotional responses. By acknowledging and understanding your emotions, you may be able to better manage them and prevent them from overwhelming you.

Increased self-awareness: Journaling can help you develop a better understanding of yourself and your inner world. As you write about your experiences and feelings, you may uncover patterns or insights that can help you better understand your motivations, desires, and values.

Stress relief: Writing can be a form of stress relief, providing a safe outlet to express your thoughts and feelings. This can help you release tension and reduce feelings of anxiety or overwhelm.

Problem solving: Writing about a problem or challenge can help you gain clarity and perspective. By putting your thoughts down on paper, you may be able to see things from a new angle and develop creative solutions to the problem.

Improved memory: Journaling can also help you remember important events or experiences. Writing about your day-to-day life or reflecting on a significant sexual event can help solidify your memories and provide a record as part of your story.

Increased creativity: Journaling can be a creative outlet, allowing you to experiment with different writing styles or explore new ideas. By giving yourself the freedom to write without judgment or constraints, you may be able to tap into new levels of creativity.

When you consider all the benefits, journaling can be an effective way to improve your emotional well-being, gain self-awareness, and explore your thoughts and feelings.

The Red Book

Carl Jung, the famous Swiss psychiatrist, kept a personal journal between 1914 and 1930. It's a highly personal and symbolic work that Jung kept private during his lifetime and was not published until after his death in 1961.

The Red Book documents Jung's exploration of his own unconscious mind, and is widely considered a key text in the development of his analytical psychology. Jung viewed the contents of *The Red Book* as a form of self-analysis and a means of connecting with his own deeper psyche.

Over the years, keeping a personal Red Book became a way to symbolize a person's exploration of the deeper sexual self. Keep your Red Book going. If you are in a stable relationship, it may be a good idea to share your Red Book with your partner. Perhaps the Red Book can be shared from the beginning so that you explore your sexual selves together. A number of my couples who are patients use a shared Red Book to secretly communicate to each other their personal fantasies. They may use it to leave notes for each other, or to suggest sexual adventures that they could explore together. Their Red Book actually becomes an important part of their sexual expression.

What have you learned about your sexual self? How have your sexual interests changed over time? Where would you like your sexual journey to go next? These are some topics for your Red Book.

Know Yourself
In conclusion, knowing your erotic profile and embracing your erotic profile is critical to achieving your best sexual self. The first secret holds a great deal of power all to itself: *Embrace Your Erotic Profile.* By understanding your own desires, preferences, and boundaries, you can develop a deeper sense of self-awareness and acceptance. This, in turn, can lead to more fulfilling intimate relationships, improved well-being, and a high level of satisfaction in life. I encourage you to take the time to explore your sexual self and embrace this important part of you. I believe it's essential to getting the most out of life and to becoming all that you can be—and that's what you want, isn't it?

Chapter Three: Your Sexual Best Is Built

In my clinical experience, I have observed that many couples do not realize that a fulfilling sexual relationship that's fun, exciting, and erotic must be built. They often do not realize that it takes time and effort, and this leads to secret number two:

Your Sexual Best Is Built

There can be no doubt, of course, thrilling sexual encounters can and sometimes do occur spontaneously—that lucky moment when you're alone in an empty bedroom at a crowded dinner party or the empty parking garage after everyone else has left the concert. Your thrill may even happen on a running trail in the great outdoors when no one else is around. Seizing those opportunities can be risky, but is certainly worth it—so why not? Most men want a sex life that is exciting, erotic, and fun—and I'm all for that. It's why I say, "Go ahead—take those opportunities when they present themselves. They are, after all, rare, why not seize the magical moments?"

Indeed, it's true, they are rare—and that's just the problem. That is why it's so important to build a fulfilling sex life that lasts. That is what this chapter is about, building something that lasts. That way when those rare magical moments do occur and you seize them, they will remain memorable.

Secrets of Men

In order to understand and fully appreciate this secret, that your best sexual self if built, you may have to let go of what you have been led to believe because of the way sex is typically portrayed in movies, porn, or erotica. I guarantee, however, that what you will discover here and experience as a result of what you learn is better than what you're getting now from the fake porn fantasies played out on your phone.

As mentioned above, an ongoing sexual relationship that's consistently fulfilling takes effort to achieve—it has to be created and fostered. Assuming that's what you want, which I'm certain you do, it's going to require work to build an environment in which sensual desire can flourish. You first need to recognize that it will take an investment of time and energy. If you commit and put your mind to it, I have no doubt that you can build a relationship that can and will deliver the sexual fulfillment you want—one that will withstand the challenges you inevitably will face as your relationship continues. After all, you're a man, and men build things. A number of authors on the subject agree that creating and building things that last is a major characteristic of masculinity.

Consider these examples:

Matthew B. Crawford: In his book, *Shop Class as Soulcraft: An Inquiry into the Value of Work,* Crawford argues that manual work, such as building, is an important part of what it means to be a man. He believes that working with your hands and creating something tangible is deeply satisfying and can help men find meaning in their lives.

Jordan B. Peterson: In his book, *12 Rules for Life: An Antidote to Chaos,* Peterson emphasizes the importance of taking responsibility and building something for yourself. He argues that building and creating are essential parts of the human experience and can help men develop a sense of purpose and direction.

Robert Bly: In his book, *Iron John: A Book About Men,* Bly explores the idea of the "wild man" archetype and how it relates to masculinity. He argues that men need to tap into their primal, instinctual nature in order to truly be fulfilled, and that building and working with their hands is one way to do this.

Brett McKay: McKay is the founder of *The Art of Manliness* website, which focuses on helping men develop traditional masculine skills and virtues. Building and DIY projects are a major focus of the site, as McKay believes that these activities can help men develop confidence and self-reliance.

Rome Wasn't Built in a Day

What took place in ancient Rome is an example that comes to mind of how men built something that has stood the test of time. The Romans needed water and by designing and building aqueducts, they were able to bring it from various mountain ranges that surrounded Rome. One of the most significant was the Apennine range, which runs the entire length of Italy—an ideal source because the mountains there receive significant rain and snowfall.

The aqueducts that brought the water were constructed during the first century AD and brought water to Rome over a distance of more than 50 miles. They were marvels of ancient technology and a testimony to the huge amount of effort that went into building them—a tremendous accomplishment that supplied water people could drink, as well as water that made the famous public baths possible. The old saying, "Rome wasn't built in a day," is true. Imagine the time and effort expended to design and build those aqueducts, as well as the public baths—not to mention other impressive structures that have stood now for two thousand years, such as the Roman Colosseum.

My point is that if you want to build an environment that's to your liking, including a healthy and fulfilling sex life, it can certainly be done, but it will require getting off the coach and spending time and effort.

What Is a Healthy Sex Life?

To begin building a satisfying sex life, let's address questions I'm often asked as a sex therapist: When it comes to sex, what's normal? How many times should we be having sex? Is it normal for me to want to do this kinky thing with my partner? Is it normal that I think about sex all the time?

As a sex therapist, I get lots of questions such as these, and I have to say that I believe the question, "Is it normal?" is not the right one. A better question is this: "Is my sex life healthy?"

It's helpful to consider what's a healthy sex life, and there are many definitions. Years ago, I found one that resonated with me. It came from John Berecz, author of *Sexual Ethics: A Theological Introduction*. He wrote that:

Sexual intimacy exists when the bio-socio-theological components of touch meld together into excitement, bonding, and creativity between the couple.

Essentially, I agree, but I have reworded his definition as follows:

A healthy sex life exists when it is mutually satisfying physically, relationally, and spiritually.

You may wish to come up with your own definition of a healthy sex life, and that's fine. No matter what yours is, however, it's critically important that sex be satisfying for both individuals involved. That's why I gravitate toward the definition above. I believe that anyone who wants to create an environment in which sex and sensuality can flourish must find ways for it to be satisfying for both the man and the woman.

Take a look at how a healthy sexual expression can be mutually satisfying physically, relationally, and spiritually:

Physically: Both participants should derive pleasure from a sexual encounter, and it ought to go beyond the physical sensations felt or the analgesic effect of endorphins being released. For example, shared sexual pleasure can and should have a positive impact on someone's self-esteem. It ought to bolster a person's confidence in his sexual abilities and desirability. Giving and receiving sexual pleasure can be a powerful way to affirm someone's self-worth, and it can lessen feelings of insecurity and foster a sense of connection and intimacy.

All the positive benefits derived from a sexual relationship should be shared by both partners. Ensuring that it's mutually satisfying physically enables all the positive benefits to flow to both of you.

Relationally: Sexual pleasure can benefit a relationship in several ways. For example, the encounter should be relationship affirming by increasing the emotional intimacy between partners. To put this another way, engaging in sex can foster a sense of closeness, connection, and vulnerability that can lead to a more meaningful relationship. When sex is mutually satisfying, it stimulates a deeper level of understanding and appreciation for one another, which can lead to an increase in satisfaction with the relationship. To achieve this requires engaging in a high degree of communication and negotiation between the two of you. By working together to identify and satisfy each other's needs and desires, you can develop a better understanding and appreciation of one another. Needless to say, when sex is mutually satisfying, it serves as a boon for the relationship.

Spiritually: Sexual expression should be affirming of both partners' spiritual values. The connection between sex and spirituality is complex and multifaceted and a subject that has been explored by many different religions and spiritual traditions throughout history. While the specific ways in which sex can affirm a person's spirituality will vary depending on individual beliefs and values, there are some general ways in which sex can be seen as a spiritual experience. Sex can be viewed as a way to connect with another on a deep and intimate level. Touch can foster a sense of empathy, compassion, and shared purpose. Sex can also be seen as a way to tap into the divine or the transcendent. It can be a powerful way to connect with another and to cultivate a deeper sense of gratitude and purpose.

Sex That's Unhealthy

I suspect you likely would be able to list a number of ways sex can be unhealthy. Perhaps you have even experienced some unhealthy expressions of sex in your relationship. These and other unhealthy sexual expressions take place when sex is not mutually satisfying physically, relationally, or spiritually. It's important to be aware of them and to avoid unhealthy sexual expressions that can cause:

Physical harm: Sexual activity can result in physical harm, such as sexually transmitted infections (STIs), unwanted pregnancies, and physical injuries.

Emotional distress: Sexual activity can cause emotional distress, including feelings of guilt, shame, or regret. This can be particularly true for those who have engaged in sexual activity they did not want, as well as for those who have been victims of sexual abuse or assault.

Relationship problems: Sexual activity can lead to relationship problems, including jealousy, betrayal, and breakups. It can also lead to conflict if one partner wants more or less sexual activity than the other.

Exploitation: Sexual activity can be exploitative, particularly when one partner has power or influence over the other. This can lead to feelings of coercion, manipulation, or abuse.

Cultural stigma: Sexual activity can be negatively viewed in some cultures or societies, leading to social ostracism or punishment. This can be particularly true for those who engage in non-heterosexual or non-monogamous sexual activity.

Legal consequences: Sexual activity can have legal consequences, particularly if one partner is underage or if sexual activity takes place without the other's consent. This can lead to criminal charges and other legal problems.

Personal values: Sexual activity can conflict with personal values and beliefs, leading to inner turmoil and psychological distress.

Spiritual/Religious beliefs: Sexual activity can conflict with spiritual or religious beliefs, leading to feelings of guilt or shame.

How Satisfied Are You Today with Your Sex Life?

To see what you may need to work on, I've developed what I call "The Sex Satisfaction Quiz" to help my clients gauge their level of satisfaction with different aspects of their sexual relationship with their partner. It is designed to stimulate conversation between the two of you and is constructed around the principle that sex is more than physical pleasure. As noted above, healthy sexual expression is based upon mutual satisfaction: physically, relationally, and spiritually. Difficulties in a couple's sex life are usually more complicated than simply adding a new twist. Sex is a physical, relational, and spiritual experience for both partners. Any dissatisfaction or difficulty in a couple's sex life could be the result of an issue in one or more of these areas. The quiz is meant to assist by identifying areas of concern.

Secrets of Men

I encourage you and your partner to take the inventory separately and then talk about the results. Complete the inventory and record your results in the appropriate field on a separate sheet of paper. The higher the number for each section the better. Lower numbers indicate potential concerns—areas you or your partner may need to work on.

Sex Satisfaction Quiz

The following inventory serves as a conversation tool for couples regarding three important aspects of a healthy sex life: physical, relational, and spirituality.

Instructions: Using the scale provided, indicate your level of agreement for the following statements. Leave statements that do not apply to your gender blank.

Completely Disagree	Somewhat Disagree	Neutral	Somewhat Agree	Completely Agree
1	2	3	4	5

1. I find sex with my partner satisfying. _____
2. I trust my partner. _____
3. I believe my sex life enriches my spiritual life. _____
4. Sex with my partner is pleasurable. _____
5. I can talk to my partner about my sexual interests. _____
6. Sex is for pleasure as well as for reproduction. _____
7. I do not have trouble getting or maintaining arousal. _____

8. My partner encourages exploration of my sexuality. _____
9. Our sexual experiences are life-giving. _____
10. I reach climax regularly with my partner. _____
11. My partner is open to fulfilling my sexual desires. _____
12. My spirituality encourages me to explore my sexuality. _____
13. I find my partner sexually arousing. _____
14. I can relax during sex. _____
15. Sexual fantasies are a normal part of my sexuality. _____
16. I desire sex with my spouse. _____
17. I can talk about sex with my spouse. _____
18. My sex life is in harmony with my spiritual life. _____
19. I feel that nothing is lacking in my sex life. _____
20. I believe that my partner can meet my sexual desires. _____
21. Sex with my partner is a spiritual act. _____
22. I am satisfied with the amount of foreplay involved in our sex. _____
23. Our relationship is strong outside the bedroom. _____
24. My spiritual life encourages me to enjoy our bodies. _____
25. Our sex life is fun. _____

Secrets of Men

25. My partner initiates sex often enough for me.

    _____

26. My sex life enhances my spiritual life. _____

27. I do not experience unwanted pain during sex.

    _____

28. I feel loved and supported by my partner.

    _____

29. I am looking forward to sex with my partner.

    _____

If you are planning to share your answers with your partner, I suggest you complete the second part of this quiz, which you will find on the next page, on a separate sheet of paper.

Secrets of Men

Sex Satisfaction Quiz
Nicholas A. Natale, PhD

Instructions: Record each response for the corresponding statement in the space provided below. Add the total from each column.

Physical Aspect. The physical aspect reflects the perceived physical pleasure experienced and the degree of satisfaction within the couple's sexual activities.

Statement Number	Response	Statement Number	Response
1.		16.	
4.		19.	
7.		22.	
10.		25.	
13.		28.	
Total		Total	

Physical Total _____

Relational Aspect. The relational aspect reflects the degree of perceived affirmation of trust and openness by the shared sexual activity.

Statement Number	Response	Statement Number	Response
2.		17.	
5.		20.	
8.		23.	
11.		26.	
14.		29.	
Total		Total	

Relational Total _____

Spiritual Aspect. The spiritual aspect reflects the individual's beliefs concerning sex from their spiritual perspective.

Statement Number	Response	Statement Number	Response
3.		18.	
6.		21.	
9.		24.	
12.		27.	
15.		30.	
Total		Total	

Spiritual Total _____

Copyright 2023 © Nicholas A. Natale. All Rights Reserved.

Communication Versus Incompatibility

Now that we understand what a healthy expression of sex can look like, let's explore how this might play out in practical ways between you and your partner. Keep in mind that the key aspect of healthy sex is that it's mutually satisfying. That being the case, it's important to realize that individuals often come to a sexual encounter with different sexual desires in mind. Although many couples are sexually compatible, even compatible partners will have days when each of them will want to experience something different in the sexual encounter. The truth is that it's rare that a couple is perfectly matched sexually all the time.

It's not uncommon for one partner in the relationship to desire a certain style of sex while the other may want something completely different on a given day. They may both be looking forward to coming together, but each may want something different. This can become a major issue. For example, one of them may have had a rough day. For the purpose of the example, let's say it's the guy. He may be stressed out from work—all he's looking for from sex that night is an orgasmic release, a quickie. Now consider that on the same night, his partner wants something completely different. She's hoping for a slow, warm, loving and connecting encounter. What do you suppose will happen when neither of them has communicated what they are looking for that night? It's not likely to go well, right? I suspect both will leave the encounter not feeling satisfied. This isn't an issue of incompatibility. It's just that they both wanted something different. Don't mistake a lack of communication for incompatibility. In the example above, it's simply a misalignment.

One of the ways that I help couples address this misalignment is through a concept called Sexual Channels. The purpose of Sexual Channels is to help couples know what they are looking for from the sexual encounter and to provide an easy way to communicate what they want to their partner. Building a thriving environment where sex can flourish involves giving and receiving touch as well as communicating. As in many areas of the relationship, this may require a certain amount of negotiation and compromise.

Think of it this way. Suppose the two of you are in the process of deciding on which restaurant to go to tonight. You might want Italian, but she may be in the mood for Mexican. She may give in, or you might give in—and if you give in, it might not be your favorite type of food. Or maybe the two of you will compromise and settle on Chinese—that might be the best solution. In a loving relationship, it's important to strive to attain mutual satisfaction—to balance giving and receiving—and that means it's all right to voice what you prefer, talk about it, and decide on something you both can agree upon.

Suppose you hear about something you have never done before, and you want to try it? For example, several years ago grapefruiting became a popular thing to try—which involves cutting the ends off a grapefruit, making a hole in the middle, putting it over the penis and going to town. It's supposed to feel like receiving oral sex and having intercourse at the same time. So, you tell your partner about this new, innovative way of having sex and you see if she'd be willing to give it a try—in other words, "Let's have some fun tonight. Let's experiment with this thing!" Trying new things; experimenting with a new sexual technique is different from a slow burning, romantic sexual encounter. If she's looking for a deep, romantic connection that night, the grapefruiting idea probably isn't what she had in mind. It may not fly with her. This is where understanding different Sexual Channels can be helpful.

Sex is large enough to include a variety of sexual expressions. On any given day when you're looking forward to being together, you may have something in mind that you would like to do with your partner. It might be a slow romantic encounter in which emotions are deeply felt, during which there's an expression of vulnerability and openness during sex. That's one particular style of sex, a specific Sexual Channel. There are literally dozens of potential Sexual Channels between each and every couple.

The bottom line is that you both need to be on the same page if you're going to connect to the fullest. The way to do that is to ensure that you and your partner are on the same Sexual Channel. To do this, you need to decide what you want and then communicate it to your partner. You can do that by letting her know what channel you're on, to which she can either agree, negotiate, or offer a compromise.

Sexual Channels

Sex is broad enough to accommodate a number of Sexual Channels. What's coming is not meant as an exhausted list—it's only meant to provide you with a sample of the possibilities. I encourage you to develop your own list and, of course, to add to it over time. Your sexual interest can change as you develop into a more experienced lover.

I also encourage you to write down the sexual channels that resonate with you. Journal entries in your Red Book could include the different channels that you enjoy the most, or that you desire to experiment with in the future. Here are some examples:

1. Romantic
2. A quickie for orgasmic release
3. Rough sex
4. Experimenting with something new
5. Drunk or high sex
6. Role-playing
7. BDSM
8. Kink play
9. Tantric sex
10. _____
11. _____
12. _____

Know Your Channels

I suggest you start by identifying your own sexual channels. In other words, what are the different types of sex that you like? I'm amazed at how many people approach sex either with anxiety, which causes their minds to race, or they can be so focused on what their partner may want that they have lost touch with what they want. I cannot overemphasize this: To achieve satisfaction and fulfillment during sexual encounters with the one that you love, you must first know what you want from the encounter. As we will see in another chapter, knowing what you want is essential for conveying and achieving confidence between you and your partner.

It's also important to know your default Sexual Channels. Usually, a person will have two or three go-tos. You might have a kinky one that, for example, involves tying her up. Your partner may not be into that all that much, but she may be willing to go along with it because she knows it's a turn-on for you. However, keep in mind, you have to know what you want before you can communicate it to her.

Communicating Your Channels

How do you broach the subject the first time? Once you identify what you want and like, you need to record it in your erotic journal. Hopefully you share your journal with your partner as was suggested in the last chapter. Then you can talk about it with her, and find ways to easily communicate it. Try to get it down to an emoji if you can or, at the very least, a way to express it in one or two words so that your partner will understand what you're in the mood for.

I've found that there are many channels. I try to get my patients to create their own and to find ways to communicate them to one another. One example that comes to mind is "TTT." A couple that was seeing me created it. I was in my office talking with this couple about Sexual Channels, and the wife looked over at her husband and said, "TTT."

He laughed.

I said, "Okay, guys. You have to tell me, what's TTT?"

She said that she discovered a couple of years ago that whenever she's on her period, her breasts become extremely sensitive. She can have an orgasm just from her husband playing with her breasts. So, she asks him to tie her up and make her orgasm by being rough with her breasts.

She said, "TTT stand for 'Tie, Titty, Tear.'"

She loves it when her husband goes after her titties during her period, especially when she's tied up. TTT is all she has to text her husband to let him know that tonight's the night. It's a channel that's unique to this couple, and that's not that unusual. Women often experience enhanced erogenous zones on various parts of their bodies at different times during their monthly cycles.

Scheduling Sex?

I'm often asked, "Is it okay to schedule sex?"

I say, "Yes, absolutely. It's a great idea."

Every couple has their own sex rhythm—the best time of day, the best day of the week, and so forth. Couples typically know when that is, so do not worry about scheduling. Often, if you schedule, you have a good opportunity to schedule a terrific sexual encounter, and it will give both of you something to look forward to.

Of course this doesn't mean you shouldn't have special, spontaneous moments. They certainly can be wonderful. Say you're in a parking garage and no one else is around. Go for it. You're on a beach at twilight, and it's deserted? Seize that moment. After all, you don't know when or if it will ever come again.

That doesn't mean, however, that your scheduled time cannot also be wonderful. It can. And so I'll repeat what I said above. Scheduling sex is perfectly okay.

In Summary

As noted at the beginning of this chapter, I have observed that many couples do not realize that a fulfilling sexual relationship that's ongoing must be built and that doing so takes time and effort. That's why the secret of this chapter is:

Your Sexual Best Is Built

You're a man, and men build things, right? Now that you have a blueprint, it's time to get started. As you move ahead, the most important thing to keep in mind is that communication is the key. The two of you need to communicate your desires, including what you're up for tonight, and sometimes one or both of you will have to compromise.

Chapter Four: Confidence Is Sexy

The goal of this chapter is to help you find and maintain your confidence during sex and at other times as well because:

Confidence Is Sexy

This is the third secret. Besides being one of the most endearing qualities a man can have—women almost universally find confident men to be particularly attractive—and when you're confident, you and your partner become more engaged with one another and more sexually stimulated. You enjoy sex more, the orgasmic experience is more powerful—and the overall experience is more satisfying. To repeat, confidence is sexy, and that's what this chapter is about.

First, let's explore the source of confidence. How can you get it, or if you have it already, how can you increase your level of confidence?

Nature Versus Nurture

A male wolf by nature is a powerful and vicious fighter that is obviously a very confident creature—unmatched by any other animal in its ecosystem. However, in recent years it has become known that, contrary to popular belief, the male wolf that leads the pack—the alpha wolf—has not fought and conquered the other males in order to attain his position. The truth is that each pack has only one alpha male and one alpha female that breed and mate for life. The two produce a new litter each year, which initially forms and then subsequently maintains their pack. The male wolf—as powerful and confident as he may be—follows the path that nature has set out for him. That's what enables him to achieve mastery of his domain, and so you might say, a male wolf is confident by nature.

We humans are not. Nature doesn't bestow confidence on us. Unlike a wolf, a man is not programmed by instinct. A man must use his intellect, and he must exert effort to achieve mastery. That's important to know and necessary to do because mastery is what leads to confidence. For a male of the human species, the ability to gain mastery over himself and to master the skills required to excel at chosen tasks are what's required. Simply put, success in the form of mastery breeds confidence.

Why Confidence Is Crucial

Unfortunately, men often silently struggle with a variety of sexual issues that can be symptomatic of a lack of confidence. For example, Erectile Dysfunction is prevalent among 50 percent of all men. In addition, Male Hypoactive Sexual Disorder (HSDD), a condition characterized by a lack of sexual desire, fantasy, or activity, is prevalent in from 15 to 25 percent. Premature Ejaculation (PE), which is when undesired ejaculation occurs within one minute of penetration at least 75% of the time, is prevalent in somewhere between 20 and 30 percent. Researchers and therapists in the field of sexual health recognize that psychological and emotional confidence is typically the number one key to effectively addressing and overcoming every one of these issues. Moreover, even if you do not suffer from any of these issues, gaining mastery over your own sexual performance will lead to a much better and more fulfilling sex life.

When you lack confidence in your touch, in your erection, in your performance, a disappointing haze is cast over the entire sexual experience, and the result is often a lackluster feeling of discontent. She may say something like, "Hey, it's okay, don't worry about it, really," but the truth is you both will likely worry about it a great deal. If you don't address it, a more disastrous situation can form that separates you from the one you love. When confidence plummets, anxiety typically takes hold. Once anxiety has a grip, a cruel cycle begins—The Anxiety Performance Trap.

The Anxiety Performance Trap

8. Just about every man has experienced an occasional sexual encounter when he wasn't able to perform. It's normal—if it happens to you, do not worry about it. Maybe it was your first time with the woman and you were nervous. Or you might have been focused on trying a new technique. Maybe you were in a different or unusual setting. Perhaps you were simply exhausted at the end of a difficult day. Such things happen, and in general, they are nothing to worry about. Next time you have an opportunity, everything is likely to go fine.

However, once anxiety contributes to your inability to perform a couple of times in a row, a dangerous cycle may form. Two or three unsatisfying experiences often are enough for the seed of doubt to grow. You might start worrying, "What if it happens again? What if I can't get it up?"

Such thoughts coupled with fear, hesitation and uncertainty can lead to another failed erection. Eventually such thoughts and emotions will become self-fulfilling. This may cause you to think something is physically wrong with you. Unless action is taken to expunge that mental baggage, it will continue to steal from you what once had been a fund and exciting time.

Someone caught in the Anxiety Performance Trap, often makes excuses concerning why sex isn't happening the way he wants, such as, "I'm not really into it tonight." "She's not turning me on anymore." "I must be getting old." "This is natural, right?" He begins to downplay the sensual part of his relationship. Afraid to pursue his intimate partner, he acts less romantic towards her. Perhaps he seeks out porn to falsely prove to himself that there's nothing actually wrong.

If that's you, blaming your partner for some perceived slight in her sexual prowess is an attempt to cover up what you know deep down to be true: there's a problem that needs to be addressed, and it's not going away on its own.

When shame, embarrassment, and disappointment are added to the mix, your sense of self-worth is going to take a hit. I have personally worked with men who have gone ten plus years without addressing the problem. They usually only come to see me when their wives finally threaten to leave them due to a grossly unsatisfying sex life.

Does it have to be this way? No, of course it doesn't. What you want is to be able to confidently share your sexual self with your lover whenever and however you'd like, and you can be that type of lover. You can perform how and when you want, and the following steps can get you there.

But I must warn you. This will not be a quick and easy fix. There is no silver bullet that will solve the problem immediately. To gain mastery over your own sexual performance, you must see what we will shortly be getting into as a process, and you will have to do the work to get through it. Some of what is contained in the upcoming steps will require you to completely flip the script concerning what you think about sex.

Let's Begin the Process

So let us begin. To remind you of what a healthy sexual encounter looks like, consider the following definition, which was expounded upon in Chapter Three:

A healthy sex life exists when it is mutually satisfying physically, relationally, and spiritually.

Note that the key is: "mutually satisfying." This means that both of you are satisfied with what is taking place. You are not there to simply perform for her, or to be the giver while she remains the receiver of pleasure. Sexual encounters that are healthy, powerful, and memorable are those during which you both experience a great deal of pleasure. Both of you need to be givers and receivers of pleasure. Your pleasure during sex matters. Building confidence in your sexual performance begins when you own what you want from the encounter. Far too often, I hear men say that their focus during sex is to satisfy her. I get that. You want to make her happy. You know somewhere deep within the recesses of your lizard brain that if she's satisfied during sex, then she's far more likely to want more sex with you. She will see you as more masculine—more manly. That's true, but it is only part of the story.

Why Confidence Is So Important

As mentioned above, confidence is attractive. She is far more likely to want more sex with you if you know and convey what you want from the sexual encounter.

Second, confidence helps you read her desires. A good lover that focuses on what he wants from the encounter is in a much better place to read and respond to what she is looking for and wants. Being confident will place you in the best position to make adjustments as the encounter unfolds.

Third, confidence is contiguous. She will be more willing to openly share what she craves when she picks up on your confident energy. She will become more confident when she realizes you are comfortable with yourself.

Exercises

Through the rest of this chapter you will have opportunities to complete exercises and apply what you're learning. Each opportunity builds upon the foundation of the previous one. Together, they form a powerful series of exercises that can significantly change your sexual experience.

Opportunity One: Explore Your Ideal Sexual Encounter

Journaling can be a helpful way to explore and clarify your thoughts and feelings about your ideal sexual encounter. Here's an exercise to get started:

Set-Up

1. *Find a quiet space:* Find a quiet and comfortable space where you won't be interrupted or distracted.
2. *Set the mood:* Light some candles, put on some relaxing music, or do anything else that helps you feel relaxed and comfortable.

Reflect

3. *Start writing:* Start by writing down what you would consider to be your ideal sexual encounter. Be as detailed and specific as possible. Some things you may want to consider include:

> Who would you be with?
> Where would you be?
> What would you be wearing?
> What kind of activities would you engage in?
> What would your partner(s) be like?
> What emotions or feelings would you want to experience?
> What kind of communication would you want to have?

4. *Explore your desires:* As you write, allow yourself to explore your desires and fantasies without judgment or inhibition. Write down everything that comes to mind, even if it seems unrealistic or unlikely.

5. *Reflect on your values:* As you write, also consider your values and what is important to you in a sexual encounter. Think about what kind of boundaries you would want to set and what kind of communication and consent would be necessary for you to feel comfortable and safe.

Intention

6. *Revisit and revise:* After you have finished writing, take some time to revisit what you've written and revise it as needed. You may find that as you reflect on your desires and values, your ideal sexual encounter may change or become more refined.

This exercise is simply a tool to help you explore your thoughts and feelings about your ideal sexual encounter. It's important to always communicate openly and honestly with a sexual partner about your desires and boundaries, and to prioritize safety and consent in any sexual encounter.

Performance Versus Pleasure

As discussed in Chapter One, men are fixers by nature. We build things. We create wonders. We make shit happen, and when we encounter a problem, we work hard to overcome it. So, when it comes to sexual performance issues such as Erectile Dysfunction, we typically double down on our remarkable ability to power through it. We try to fix it by being better, trying harder—doing more.

Wrong! Wrong! Wrong! That is a sure-fire way of stepping into the Anxiety Performance Trap. Your outer world is a reflection of your inner world, and so to change your outer world, you must first change your inner world. Replace your anxiety with the picture you created above—your ideal sexual encounter. Once you do, the problem that's been created by your anxiety and self-doubt will disappear.

When it comes to performance issues in the bedroom, focusing on making something happen, forcing something to happen, is the wrong approach. It only exacerbates the problem. Trying harder releases stress chemicals in the brain and that are not conducive to getting and maintaining an erection. When you're so focused on making something happen, it releases adrenaline hormones into the body and this channels blood flow to your outer extremities—namely your hands if you're more of the fighter type, or to your legs if you're a flight type of person. Either way, you're not sending the blood flow to your core.

In a sexual encounter, you must focus more on the pleasure you're receiving and giving—focus on pleasure, not performance. Pleasure is relaxing, calming, relieving. The goal is to reach your Pleasure Zone. When that becomes your inner world it will be mirrored in your outer world.

The Pleasure Zone

The Pleasure Zone is an erotic headspace. It's that place of calm you can achieve when your mind is quiet—everything seems to slow down a little, and you enjoy being erotic and present in the pleasure of the moment. That's when you will not be distracted by racing thoughts that are fueled by fear—worried that something will go wrong. In the Pleasure Zone, your attention increasingly focuses on the sensations you are experiencing as your hand caresses her body and you feel the warmth of her. You sense your body responding and her body responding. You might experience the taste of her lingering on your lips, or the smooth curve of her buttocks against your body. Just let it happen—enter the Pleasure Zone as you begin to feel the growing power of arousal take its shape. This is a place you can learn to slip into naturally, anytime, and every time. It's a place where nothing else matters except satisfying your growing need.

The problem is that a lot of guys cannot reach The Pleasure Zone because they are so focused on what's going on in their heads and around them—their partner's pleasure, the environment, am I doing this right, what should I do next? That's when someone's inner world gets reflected in his outer world.

Please remember that your sexual desire begins and ends with your desire. You are responsible for your sexual experience, and your lover is responsible for hers. So create a picture in your mind of what you want. If you're hyperfocused on pleasuring your partner, you won't be able to stay focused on your own desire. Simply put, if you're focused on what could go wrong, you're far from where you need to be. It's just about inevitable that you will be torpedoed by a self-fulfilling prophecy.

Opportunity Two: Focus on Your Desire

Some guys have lost touch with what turns them on. They are so focused on everything else, they can't reach their own Pleasure Zone. This exercise is about rediscovering your desires, wants, and passions.

Reflect on these questions:

- What turns you on the most?
- When you self-pleasure, where does your mind go?
- Where do you like to be touched? Kissed?
- Do you have a kink that you want to express during sex?
- How do you communicate to your partner what you want to do and to be done to you?

The Anxiety Solution

Anxiety is a natural part of the human experience. Everyone experiences it from time to time in one form or another, and so its presence does not indicate weakness or failure. The truth is that we need anxiety in order to survive and to thrive. This was particularly true for our primitive ancestors, which likely is why we inherited the tendency to be anxious. They had to live off the woods, the river, the ocean, or the sea. They rarely were certain where their next meal was coming from. They had to worry that a predator might attack them at any time. Anxiety kept them alert—it was essential to their survival.

In the twenty-first century we no longer have to worry that our family might be attacked by a pack of wolves, or that the tribe across the river might sneak up and wipe us out, so sometimes we worry about things that may not be worth the time and effort. Nevertheless, anxiety remains a reliable indicator that something isn't quite right.

As we have seen, anxiety can have a devastating effect on our sexual experiences. If you want to deal with your anxiety when it comes to performing, you need a solution that can set you free from its powerful grip. A viable solution is contained within the simple observation, "We cannot stop—we can only replace." This simple truth encompasses our behaviors, thoughts, and emotions. It speaks to the truth that we cannot arbitrarily stop a behavior, a thought, or an emotion unless we replace it with something else. How do you stop thinking about the polar bear in the living room? Replace it with something—maybe a lamp.

Think of the smoker who finally quits and then gains 20 pounds. He replaced smoking with eating more. He didn't just stop smoking. He replaced smoking with eating—not exactly a positive result. He'd have been better off to direct his attention in a different direction. Perhaps fitness or a new hobby would have been better than beer, candy, or an extra high stack of pancakes for breakfast.

Without a conscious effort, we will find something to replace a bad habit for an equally unhealthy and bad habit. The same is true for emotions. If you have an ongoing undesirable emotional response, your best solution is to be intentional about selecting a replacement.

If you want to tackle your anxiety in the bedroom, the best solution I've found is to focus on the pleasure you're experiencing during an encounter. That way, you will not be focusing on what is or is not taking place with respect to your erection. We cannot stop, we only replace. By concentrating on the pleasure you are experiencing, your mind will be less prone to conjure up thoughts that will bring on the self-fulfilling prophecy of failure.

Focus on Pleasure Not Failure

Focusing on pleasure is an intentional skill that must be practiced and mastered. This is especially true for someone caught in the Anxiety Performance Trap. That erotic headspace called the Pleasure Zone is the natural state of raw arousal that allows your body to respond. Confidence is naturally experienced in this state. This is where you want to be. And you can get there with a little practice. To focus more on pleasure, you must begin with your own hand.

Opportunity Three: Solo Touch Exercise

Here is a touch exercise to help you become more aware of the pleasure in sexual activity:

Set-Up

1. *Find a comfortable space:* Find a quiet and comfortable space where you won't be interrupted or distracted.

2. *Set the mood:* Create a relaxing and sensual atmosphere by dimming the lights, lighting candles, or putting on some soothing music.

3. *Get in a comfortable position:* Sit or lie down in a comfortable position, and take a few deep breaths to relax your body.

Experience

4. *Start touching:* Begin touching your body in a slow and gentle way, exploring different areas and noticing how your body responds. Focus on areas that feel pleasurable, such as your chest, stomach, inner thighs, or genitals.

5. *Experiment with different touches:* Try experimenting with different types of touches, such as light strokes, firm pressure, or circular movements. Notice how each type of touch feels and how your body responds.

6. *Focus on breathing:* As you touch yourself, focus on your breathing and allow yourself to fully immerse in the sensations you are experiencing.

7. *Continue exploring:* Continue exploring different areas of your body, focusing on the areas that feel most pleasurable. As you become more comfortable with the sensations, you may choose to touch yourself more directly or experiment with different techniques.

Reflect

8. *Reflect on your experience:* After you finish the exercise, take some time to reflect on your experience. Think about what you enjoyed most, what surprised you, and what you might want to explore further in future touch exercises.

This exercise is not intended to replace sexual activity with a partner, but rather to help you become more aware of your own pleasure and build confidence in your ability to experience and express pleasure, and thereby replace anxiety with the experience of sensual pleasure.

Confidence in the Bedroom

It's important to become and be a man who is aware that no matter what situation arises, you will be able to handle it. Confidence is not about controlling the narrative or controlling the situation—in other words, manipulating it towards your advantage. Confidence is about the ability to handle a situation, to adapt to it—to overcome whatever is happening. Every man should want that level of confidence in bed.

Another prime principle is that sexually confident men are comfortable with the coming and going of their erections during a sexual encounter. Confidence is about you—not your erection. Some men are so focused on their erections during sex that the slightest fluctuation with their member will completely throw them off. The loss of an erection can completely shut down some men. They pull away, retreat within themselves, and become irritated when their lover asks if everything's okay.

This is one reason some men move too fast during sexual encounters. They head straight to intercourse because they fear they'd "better use it now before it goes away." This connotes a scarcity mindset and is often met by an unhappy lover because she hasn't yet had the opportunity to build her own arousal. Slowing the scene down is better for both parties.

A confident man is able to stay present in the Pleasure Zone as he sees his erection come and go. Though it is not always taught in sex education classes, or demonstrated on the screen, an erection is designed to come and go and return again during a sexual encounter. Therefore, there is no reason to become stressed out over the loss of an erection.

Opportunity Four: A Thought Exercise

Consider this scenario and write down your answers to the questions below.

Imagine giving oral stimulation to your lover. She is enjoying your ministrations and you decide to continue until she climaxes. You're going to take her there. A few minutes into it, you notice your own erection begins to wane. You slip your hand to grip your member to try to keep it hard while you continue pleasuring her. In the process, you finally realize you're losing the battle. Your firmness is slipping away. The more you focus on her, the more you feel yourself becoming soft. Which of these options would you focus on and what goes on in your head:

1. Continuing to pleasure her, or the loss of your erection?
2. What do you begin to think and/or feel when you notice your erection going away?
3. Where does your mind go?
4. Have you ever lost your erection during sex?
5. What does that do to you emotionally?
6. What happened next during the sexual encounter? Did it end? Or did you continue to pleasure her?

A lot of guys are not comfortable with their erections coming and going during a sexual encounter. Remember the principle that confidence your erection will return will allow you to focus on the pleasure that you're receiving and giving.

Opportunity Five: The Solo Touch Exercise

To help you build confidence, this touch exercise is designed to help you see how your erection can easily come and go during a sexual encounter.

- Begin by focusing on a passionate sexual encounter that you had before. (If you have not experienced a passionate sexual encounter yet, that's okay. Make one up!)
- Self-pleasure in a way that is pleasing to you, focusing on the sensation, the pleasure of your own touch. Pleasure yourself to the point that you can feel a firm erection.
- Pause the pleasure for a moment and notice the feeling of your erection. Become aware of how it begins to decline.
- Once it is flaccid, begin to stroke it again. Self-pleasure until it is firm again.
- When it is firm a second time (without climaxing), stop pleasuring and allow your member to decline again.
- Repeat this rotation several more times.
- Enjoy the pleasure of the climax.

I hope you will consider repeating Opportunity Five above often. Doing so will help you build mastery over your erection and even enable you to control the timing of your ejaculation. The ability to become aware of when you're about the ejaculate and then take actions to prevent it will boost your confidence enormously. It can become second nature to you and thereby help you perform better.

Practice can make perfect.

Opportunity Six: Couple Sexual Touch Exercise

Now that you have worked through Opportunities One through Five, it's time to bring your partner into the program. This is a touch that you can explore together to become more aware of pleasure in sexual activity:

Set-Up

1. *Find a comfortable space:* Find a quiet and comfortable space where you won't be interrupted or distracted.

2. *Set the mood:* Create a relaxing and sensual atmosphere by dimming the lights, lighting candles, or putting on some soothing music.

3. *Get in a comfortable position:* Sit or lie down in a comfortable position together and take a few deep breaths to relax your bodies.

Experience

4. *Start touching:* Begin by exploring each other's bodies in a slow and gentle way, focusing on areas that feel pleasurable. You might start with non-sexual areas, such as the arms, back, or neck, before moving on to more erogenous zones.

5. *Experiment with different touches:* Try experimenting with different types of touches, such as light strokes, firm pressure, or circular movements. Encourage your partner to guide you and communicate what feels good to them.

6. *Focus on breathing:* As you touch each other, focus on your breathing and allow yourselves to fully immerse in the sensations you are experiencing.

7. *Continue exploring:* Continue exploring each other's bodies, focusing on the areas that feel most pleasurable. As you become more comfortable with the sensations, you may choose to touch each other more directly or experiment with different techniques.

8. *Communicate and give feedback:* Throughout the exercise, communicate openly and honestly with each other about what feels good and what you want more of. Give each other positive feedback and encouragement.

Reflect

9. *Reflect on your experience:* After you finish the exercise, take some time to reflect on your experience together. Talk about what you enjoyed most, what surprised you, and what you might want to explore further in future touch exercises or sexual activity.

This exercise is meant to be a fun and exploratory way to become more aware of each other's pleasure and to build intimacy and connection. As always, it is important to prioritize safety, communication, and consent in any sexual activity.

Where do we go from here?

The principles and intentional opportunities provided above combine to form a starting point that has proven effective with respect to journeys others have taken to arrive at being confident in bed. As with every important aspect of growth in life, the concepts are not difficult, but putting them into practice can be. Take time to practice. Own your sexual expression. Master yourself. Realize that this may require you to flip the script of what you believe about sex and cause you to look at sex from a new and different perspective. Anxiety is not your friend, but it doesn't have to be your enemy. Once you understand what you're experiencing in bed, you can begin to redirect your focus away from anxiety towards pleasure and your vision of the ideal sexual encounter. The Pleasure Zone is your key to breaking free from the Anxiety Performance Trap.

Gaining mastery of your sexual self means that you're gaining mastery over your fears. A big plus of the effort you expend is that once you attain mastery in bed, you will have more confidence in other areas of your life.

Whatever you do, keep this in mind: Confidence is sexy. Here's a true story that illustrates this.

Story Time

You can tell a lot about a man by the way he handles his dog. In my neighborhood, the dog park is a popular place. It's well-designed, sectioned into two separate areas, one for smaller dogs and the other for bigger breeds. It's shaded with large oak trees, manicured grass, and plenty of obstacles for the dogs to interact with. Usually, people bring their furry friends, let them interact with other dogs and play for a while as they watch and chat it up with their neighbors. It's a relaxed and fun way to meet other people.

One Saturday afternoon, I noticed a guy talking with three women against the fence as their dogs played. I sat and watched the four of them interact as my own shepherd played with his friends. They were enjoying a simple and pleasant conversation with each other. Occasionally, the man's puppy, a white socked border collie, would come over and check-in with her owner and then happily run back to the other dogs to play for a while longer. I could tell her owner was a confident fellow. He didn't appear to be overly stressed about his puppy—she was playing fine—he only intervened if necessary. The man was relaxed, hands in his pockets, enjoying the conversation and the company of his female neighbors. When it was time to go, he simply called his puppy, and she came right to him. He gave the command for her to sit, and she promptly obeyed. He latched the lead to her collar and the man and his dog walked away.

I couldn't help but notice how the three women subtly and positively responded to this small display of authority. They watched it unfold while glancing at each other with obvious respect for the way he was handling the excited puppy. I also noticed how they continued to watch him walk away on the sidewalk even though he never turned his head to look back at them.

It was obvious. This man's confidence had gained their attention.

Secrets of Men

Unfortunately, the same was not true for the next guy who arrived at the park. "Confident" is the antithesis of how I would describe this man's manner. He would jerk at his dog's lead and constantly call out her name in an attempt to get her to obey. He chased her around the dog park when it was time to go. No confidence was displayed by this guy—only fear, panic, and desperation. Everyone around him picked up on this. He was awkward, nervous, and over-correcting as he lost patience with his dog.

One of the women who had been part of the original group of four came over to try to help him catch his energetic pup. It was humorous to watch him attempt to start up a conversation with her. She simply wasn't interested.

You can learn a lot about a man by the way he handles his dog, which is one way to keep in mind that "confidence is sexy."

Chapter Five: Face Sexual Shame

The secret this chapter reveals is one that I've found many men do not want to talk about or think about. You might be among this group and therefore inclined to skip this chapter and move on to the next. I urge you not to do so. You may not realize it, but sexual shame might be holding you back from becoming your best sexual self, which is why I encourage you to continue reading and judge for yourself whether or not shame might be an issue for you to explore.

When I work with men who are experiencing difficulty with sexual issues, and we peel back layers of the onion in our search for the cause, I frequently learn that a patient's inhibitions and hang-ups stem from sexual shame that's hidden deep inside. It's why the secret of this chapter is so important, which is:

Face Sexual Shame.

There can be no doubt about it. To become your best sexual self you must face and overcome your sexual shame. But before we go into this further, let's be sure we are on the same page about the meaning of the word, "shame." People often believe that the words "guilt" and "shame" are synonymous. They are not. It's true they are related—both are emotions that have to do with actions that are wrong, but the implications of these two words are distinctly different.

Guilt is a feeling of remorse or regret for behavior or an act that the person who feels guilt realizes he should not have done. Guilt focuses on the behavior and the impact the behavior had on others. The truth is guilt can be a healthy emotion because it can motivate someone to apologize and to make amends. Because we feel guilty, we are able to learn from our mistakes, make positive changes, and thereby not make similar errors in the future.

Shame, on the other hand, has to do with how someone feels about himself. It is a more complex and often much more deeply rooted emotion than guilt. To feel shame is to consider oneself to be unworthy or flawed in some way. That's very different from feeling regret or remorse about having done something you wish you hadn't. You feel guilty because you made a mistake or have behaved badly in a particular circumstance, but having done so does not make you a permanently flawed human being.

Shame can have an extremely negative impact on a person's sense of self-worth. Feelings of unworthiness due to shame are often fueled and exasperated by self-criticism, negative self-talk, and societal or cultural messages that one takes seriously and internalizes.

In summary, guilt tells me that I have done something wrong. Shame tells me that there is something wrong with me. Guilt can motivate positive change, whereas shame often leads to feelings of isolation, disconnection, and self-loathing. Shame can also lead to destructive behaviors such as addiction, self-harm, and avoidance of social situations.

Here is what some of the most on the prolific authors have to say on this topic:

Secrets of Men

Guilt says I've done something wrong; shame says there is something wrong with me. Guilt says I've made a mistake; shame says I am a mistake.

—John Bradshaw,
Healing the Shame that Binds You
(Recovery Classics, 2005)

Guilt is feeling bad about what you've done. Shame is feeling bad about who you are.

—Brené Brown,
The Gifts of Imperfection: Let Go of Who You Think You're Supposed to Be and Embrace Who You Are
(Hazelden Publishing; Anniversary edition, 2022)

Shame is the most powerful, master emotion. It's the fear that we're not good enough.

—Lewis Howes,
The Mask of Masculinity: How Men Can Embrace Vulnerability, Create Strong Relationships, and Live Their Fullest Lives (Rodale Books; Reprint edition, 2019)

Guilt focuses on behavior; shame focuses on self.

—June Tangney and Ronda Dearing,
Shame and Guilt
(The Guilford Press; 1st edition, 2003)

Secrets of Men

Shame is the lie someone told you about yourself.

—Anais Nin,
Seduction of the Minotaur
(Sky Blue Press; 1st edition, 2010)

The quotations above make it clear that guilt is focused on behavior and actions, whereas shame is focused on a person's sense of self and worth. Understanding the difference between these two emotions can be important in order to work through them and move towards healing and growth.

Sexual Shame

It should go without saying that sex is a powerful and compelling part of a person's life. When sex and shame are combined in someone, the result can be extremely negative. Sexual shame often stems from negative beliefs or experiences to do with sex, and it can result from a sense of being inadequate or defective because of one's thoughts and ideas about sex, as well as one's feelings, desires, or behaviors. It often leads to a number of negative emotions and experiences, such as anxiety, fear, self-loathing, and the avoidance of sexual intimacy.

Sexual shame can be the result of a range of factors, including religious or cultural beliefs, negative experiences, body image issues, and more. It often operates well below the service and is so deeply ingrained that it may not be immediately apparent to the individual who is affected by it, but it nevertheless can have significant impacts on a person's mental health, as well as his or her relationships and overall quality of life.

Addressing and overcoming sexual shame often involves identifying and challenging negative beliefs and messages, learning to accept and love one's body and sexuality, and exploring and expressing one's sexual self in a safe and consensual manner. Doing whatever is necessary is worth the effort because overcoming and ridding oneself of sexual shame can lead to a higher level of self-acceptance, greater intimacy in relationships, and a more positive relationship with one's sexuality.

Messages from Men on Shame

In my career as a therapist, I have dealt with and worked to help quite a number of men who faced and overcame the scourge of sexual shame. The following are messages that are representative of those I have received from these men over the years. They came from guys who had finally reached the point that they wanted to deal with this issue. Each has been edited somewhat, but each reflects the individual's intended message—that he is finally ready and willing to face and overcome his shame:

> "For me, sexual shame feels like a heavy weight on my shoulders, a constant feeling of embarrassment about my own sexual desires and behaviors. It comes up in my life often. I find myself avoiding sex, even if I'm attracted to someone, because I feel like my desires are wrong. When I do have sex, I

feel guilty afterwards, even if there was nothing objectively wrong about the experience. I want to change this!" —Frank

"As a Christian, I had always felt deeply ashamed of my desires. I grew up in a religious home that taught that sex was something dirty, sinful, and shameful, and I internalized those beliefs without realizing it. For years later, I found myself avoiding sex altogether, even when I was in a relationship. When I did have sex, I felt guilty and dirty afterwards, as if I had done something wrong. I would engage in negative self-talk, criticizing myself for my sexual desires and fantasies. Eventually, I shut down my own desires." —Juan

"Imagine feeling a deep sense of guilt and self-blame after ever sexual encounter. I remember feeling this way after my first sexual experience, as though I had done something wrong or immoral. Even though I had married her and felt physically and emotionally ready, I couldn't shake the feeling that I had somehow violated her boundary. This shame manifested in my day-to-day life as a sense of unworthiness, as though I didn't deserve to have healthy sexual relationships or enjoy my own desires. It began to affect my ability to perform with my wife. I could get it up for porn, but not with her. I need help!" —Chris

Causes of Sexual Shame

There are many possible causes of sexual shame, including:

Cultural or religious beliefs: Some cultural or religious beliefs can teach that sex is shameful or dirty, especially outside of marriage.

Negative experiences: Negative sexual experiences, such as sexual assault, harassment, and trauma can create feelings of shame or guilt.

Lack of education: A lack of education about sexuality can lead to confusion and shame around sexual feelings and desires.

Personal beliefs or values: Personal beliefs or values to do with sexuality can also lead to feelings of shame, especially if they conflict with one's desires or behaviors.

Family upbringing: Family attitudes and messages around sexuality can impact how individuals view sex and their own desires.

Gender and sexuality norms: Societal norms around gender and sexuality can create shame for those who do not fit into traditional or accepted categories.

Body image issues: Negative body image or self-esteem issues can also contribute to feelings of shame around sexuality.

It's important to note that sexual shame is often influenced by a combination of these factors, and that it can be a complex and deeply ingrained emotion.

Identifying Sexual Shame

You may say, "I don't have any sexual shame." If that is true, I am sincerely happy for you, but before you totally dismiss the possibility, it's important to know that sexual shame can present itself in a variety of ways. Here are some common signs and symptoms:

Avoidance of sexual experiences: Someone experiencing sexual shame may avoid sexual experiences altogether or may engage in sexual behavior but feel guilty or ashamed about it afterwards.

Negative self-talk: A person with sexual shame may engage in negative self-talk, criticizing his own sexual desires, fantasies, or behaviors.

Body shame: Sexual shame can often be linked to body shame, with the person feeling embarrassed or ashamed of his body and its natural functions.

Fear of judgment: Someone with sexual shame may fear judgment or rejection from others if his sexual desires or behaviors were to be revealed.

Low self-esteem: Sexual shame can be linked to a broader sense of low self-esteem, with the person feeling unworthy or inadequate in his sexual identity.

Lack of intimacy: Sexual shame can lead to a lack of intimacy in romantic relationships, as the person may feel disconnected from his own sexuality and struggle to connect with their partner sexually.

RECLAIM Your Sexual Self

Sexual shame is a pervasive and often deeply ingrained emotion that can significantly impact your overall well-being, self-esteem, and relationships. Fortunately, however, there is an effective approach to address and work through your sexual shame.

RECLAIM is an acronym for a comprehensive approach that provides individuals with a step-by-step process for working through and overcoming shame. The model is based on six principles, each of which is represented by a letter in the word, RECLAIM. I learned this approach from Kaz Riley, a fantastic sex educator, hypnotist, and founder of "Sexual Freedom Hypnosis" (https://sexualfreedomhypnosis.org/) based in the United Kingdom.

Recognize the shame: The first step in addressing sexual shame is to recognize and acknowledge its presence. This involves identifying the thoughts, emotions, and physical sensations that are associated with shame.

Evaluate the sources and origins: It's important to uncover where the shame came from. The source could be negative messages about sex from family, culture, and religion.

Courage to challenge and change: Challenging those negative beliefs and messages is the third step. This involves you directly questioning the beliefs and messages with what you know to be true about your desires, sex, and sexuality.

Let the past belief go: This involves you identifying exceptions about sex and intimacy so that you can begin to move past the old beliefs.

Accept the new belief and learning: Practicing acceptance of your experiences is the fifth step. This involves learning to accept your sexuality and your history with sexual shame without judgment or criticism.

Move forward: This step involves integrating the experience of sexuality into your life story in a more positive and adaptive way. This can involve reframing past experiences in a more positive light and developing a new narrative around your sexuality.

The RECLAIM process can effectively help you find new ways to embrace what has happened in the past and discover what is possible in the future. Is not an easy path to follow for most people with sexual shame, but the word is priceless and the process worth the effort. You may need help and assistance with it from a counselor or coach. Do not be afraid to reach out for help if you are dealing with sexual shame.

How to Become the Best Sexual You

Thank you for reading this chapter all the way to the end. I hope you found it to be informative and helpful—whether or not it brought to the surface the possibility that you may have a sense of sexual shame that needs to be addressed. The goal of this book is for you to become your best sexual self, and if shame is an issue, the secret revealed in this chapter—*Face Sexual Shame*—is one to take seriously. You must look at that negative baggage hidden away in your psyche square in the face, recognize where it came from, realize it's nothing but a lot of BS, and shoo it away.

Chapter Six: Porn Conditions You

I am the embodiment of the primal desires within,
Fulfilling and unsatisfying, a paradoxical sin.
My veil is opaque, yet I'm ubiquitous in plain sight,
A mirror reflecting the shadow, both shadow and light.
My power comes from the taboo, from what's not allowed,
A feast for the senses, yet with consequences, avowed.
My worshippers often see me as a portal to the divine,
A way to transcend, to unite with the sublime.
But be wary, my friend, for I'm a Pandora's box,
Opening me can unleash chaos, pain, and paradox.
I'm porn, the force that's both dark and bright,
The forbidden fruit, the ecstasy, the endless night.

The Secret

The secret this chapter addresses is one many men do not want to talk about or even think about. It's based on the fact that the regular use of pornography can condition a man to the point that he is unable to perform as he would like with a human intimate partner. When searching for the root cause of sexual performance issues, I often find that inabilities stem from the regular use of porn. That being so, simply stated, here is the secret this chapter reveals:

Secrets of Men

Porn Conditions You

The result is that to become your best sexual self you must overcome your desire to use pornography and recondition your body's arousal mechanism to respond to the stimuli present in a normal sexual encounter.

The Endless Night

Pornography has become more accessible than ever before, with the widespread availability of the Internet and many different devices and platforms on which to view it. While pornography can be a source of pleasure and arousal for some, it can also have negative effects on a man's ability to perform sexually with a partner. In this chapter, we will explore some of the ways that porn use can negatively impact a person's natural arousal response as well as the top reasons why a person returns to porn again and again, and, finally, how to find mastery over porn.

How about you? Do you watch pornography? Do you do so frequently? If so, the result could be that the effects of doing so may be keeping you from becoming your sexual best. In my line of work as a sex therapist, the negative effects pornography can have on the sexual performance of a regular user is a hot topic. Many in my field see pornography as an addition. Others disagree and are almost disgusted by the term because they see it as an attempt to repress or shame those with an interest in sex who use pornography to explore it. I do not believe that it is or that it can be an addiction. But based on patients I have treated, I have found that regular use of porn can create and perpetuate a problem. Some people become what might be considered "trapped" by pornography to the point that it negatively affects their sexual performance. But that doesn't mean they are addicted.

Sexual arousal is the body's natural response to sexual stimuli, which involves a complex interplay of physical and psychological factors that work together to produce feelings of pleasure that prepare the body for sex. However, the use of pornography can interfere with this natural process in a number of ways that we will explore in this chapter. But first, we have to get something out of the way first—the debate concerning whether or not porn is addictive.

Porn Addiction Versus Porn Conditioning

There is a simmering debate between sex therapists, researchers, and other healers about the term "porn addiction." For years, the term has been a relevant and descriptive way to describe the condition of someone who experiences the compulsory use of pornography. The debate around pornography and addiction is a complex and ongoing one, with differing opinions and perspectives often being expressed by various authors and experts. Broadly speaking, some authors see porn as an addiction, while others do not.

Those who view it as an addiction argue that the compulsive use of porn can have negative consequences on individuals, such as changes in brain chemistry, increased tolerance, withdrawal symptoms, and difficulty controlling the use of porn. They suggest that like other addictive substances or behaviors, porn use can be a source of distress and can interfere with one's daily life and relationships. They often advocate for treatment options and support groups to help individuals who are struggling with excessive porn use.

Suffice it to say that if someone is addicted, it means their body needs or craves whatever it is they are addicted to. A heroin addict, for example, may not be able to get a full night's sleep because his body will wake him up because it needs a heroin "fix." In such a case, his body is physically addicted. In my opinion, that doesn't actually happen with porn. I believe the primary problem with porn is that someone can become so "conditioned" by it that traditional sex with a human partner becomes difficult and sometimes impossible.

Some authors do not view porn as addictive. They see it as a personal choice and a form of entertainment. They argue that while excessive porn use can be problematic for some, it is not inherently addictive in the way some substances such as drugs or alcohol can be. They suggest that individuals should have the freedom to choose whether or not to use pornography, and that excessive porn use may be better understood as a symptom of underlying issues, rather than an addiction in and of itself. It's worth noting that there is ongoing debate and discussion around this issue, with many experts holding nuanced and complex views on the relationship between porn and addiction. Below are some statements by authors on each side of this issue.

Secrets of Men

Authors who see porn as an addiction:

"Pornography addiction, which is a subset of sex addiction, is a serious problem that has received increasing attention in recent years."

—Alexandra Katehakis,
author of *Sex Addiction as Affect Dysregulation*

"People are getting hooked on porn in ways that are similar to the ways that people get hooked on drugs."

—Gary Wilson,
author of *Your Brain on Porn: Internet Pornography and the Emerging Science of Addiction*

"Pornography addiction is a relatively new concept, but it is increasingly recognized as a real and serious problem."

—Kevin Skinner,
author of *Treating Pornography Addiction: The Essential Tools for Recover*

Turn the page to see what authors say who do not see porn as an addiction:

"Pornography is not the problem. It's the shame, guilt, and repression surrounding sexuality that create the problem."

—Esther Perel, author of *Mating in Captivity: Unlocking Erotic Intelligence*

"Pornography is not inherently addictive, but it can be used compulsively or excessively, which can lead to problems."

—Marty Klein, author of *America's War on Sex: The Attack on Law, Lust, and Liberty*

"Porn is a choice, not an addiction. And like all choices, it should be made freely, without coercion or shame."

—Pamela Paul, author of *Pornified: How Pornography Is Damaging Our Lives, Our Relationships, and Our Families*

Whether or not you hold a strong opinion one way or another in this debate is completely up to you. Both sides are out to help individuals who struggle with the problem of porn and its negative effects on their lives and relationships.

My larger concern here is how porn can condition an individual who is sexually stimulated regularly while he is alone with a screen. This can lead to significant negative issues when the individual has a sexual encounter with an actual person. In other words, a person can become so conditioned by using porn that it negatively affects his ability to realize his full sexual potential when with an actual sexual partner.

Yes, there is such a thing as "Porn Conditioned."

What Exactly Is Conditioning?

Humans and their bodies can and do become conditioned in many ways, such as when and how much we eat and when during a twenty-four hour period we typically have a bowel movement. A person's body who works the night shift at a factory or the Seven Eleven can become conditioned to sleep during the day and stay awake at night. If you have ever taken a flight to Europe or the Far East and experienced jet lag, you know that prior to that trip your body had become conditioned to waking up and going to sleep at times that aren't compatible with your new location. After a few days your body will become conditioned to the new time zone, which means you will no doubt experience jet lag again when you return home. This indicates, of course, that conditioning can be overcome.

The ability for the human body to be conditioned is what's behind the negative effect porn can have on the ability to have satisfying sex with a human partner. Imagine that someone frequently watches pornography and pleasures himself to the point of ejaculation. If he does this often enough, he is unconsciously conditioning his body's arousal response mechanism. This is why the biggest potential problem with pornography is not whether it's addictive or problematic behavior, but rather, how it can condition someone to respond to sexual stimuli.

Watching porn and pleasuring oneself is a totally different experience than a sexual encounter with a partner. The result can be that a regular user of porn may no longer have the ability to have satisfying sex a real human being because he may not be able to become aroused and respond as he would like. I have a name for this. I call it, "15 to one." Let me say parenthetically that this is not based on a scientific study. It's based on what as a sex therapist I have observed.

Athletes Condition Their Bodies to Perform

To make the point about conditioning, an analogy I use is that of an NFL football receiver working out prior to a game. He gets in his stance. He runs his route, and he catches the ball. He does this over and over because he wants it to become automatic. He's building muscle memory. He doesn't want to have to think about what to do every time he goes out for a pass during the game.

Now imagine someone who has sex with a screen 15 times for every one time with a real person. His body has very likely become conditioned by that activity with a screen so that when he is with a person, he's a little like a fish out of water. He doesn't know exactly what to do or how to do it.

Secrets of Men

Think for a moment how porn is typically experienced. Let's say it's been a while and a guy feels the need for release. Maybe he's at work or school so he makes plans and decides on a time when he can go online—a time when he can be completely alone. The time comes and he pulls up PornHub. He can search through thousands of categories and choose the video he wants to watch. He selects one based on a number of different parameters—the actors, the thumbnail, the description, how many likes it has, whatever captures his imagination. It's totally up to him which one he selects.

He starts watching, and at some point he begins to stimulate himself through self-pleasure. He does so at the firmness and the rhythm he prefers—suffice it to say he is in complete control of the entire experience. When he's done—when he has ejaculated—he cleans up. He may hide his activity by doing what's required to erase his online activity. Finally, now that he's all done, he may feel a bit of guilt, shame, or embarrassment about what he just did.

My point is that the entire experience is completely different than sex with a female partner. He was in control from beginning to end, and when it's over, the emotional experience was negative. Imagine that's someone's experience 15 times for every one time with a real partner. That individual may well have become conditioned by that type of sex. It doesn't matter if it's called an addiction or problematic behavior. My concern is how it can negatively affect someone's ability to perform with a partner or spouse. That's the premise of the work I do with men and women when it comes to this issue.

Let me summarize how porn use can negatively affect a person's natural arousal response. It does so by desensitizing him to sexual stimuli. When a person views porn regularly, he can become accustomed to the intense sexual stimuli that it presents. This can make it more difficult for him to become aroused by less intense sexual stimuli, such as touch or kissing. Moreover, this desensitization can, over time, lead to a decrease in sexual desire and an inability to experience pleasure and arousal.

Porn use can also lead to a reduction in the brain's response to natural sexual stimuli. Research has shown that when a person views porn, it can activate the same reward pathways in the brain as drugs such as cocaine and heroin. This can lead to a decrease in the brain's response to natural sexual stimuli, as the brain becomes more accustomed to the intense reward signals provided by porn. This is what can make it more difficult for a person to become aroused.

On top of that, porn use can lead to a decrease in the sensitivity of the genitals. This can occur when a person engages in excessive masturbation or uses sex toys excessively. When a person becomes accustomed to the intense stimulation provided by these activities, it can become more difficult for them to become aroused during sexual activity with a partner. This can lead to feelings of frustration and shame and can ultimately lead to a decrease in sexual desire and an inability to experience pleasure and arousal during sexual activity.

Finally, porn use can negatively affect a person's emotional response to sexual stimuli. When a person views porn, he may become accustomed to the unrealistic sexual scenarios and body types that it presents. This can lead to feelings of inadequacy and shame, as he may feel that he is unable to live up to those unrealistic standards. This can lead to a decrease in sexual desire and an inability to experience pleasure and arousal during sexual activity because the person's emotional response to sexual stimuli has been negatively impacted.

In summary, porn use can have a number of negative effects on a person's natural arousal response. It can lead to desensitization to sexual stimuli, a reduction in the brain's response to natural sexual stimuli, a decrease in the sensitivity of the genitals, and a negative impact on a person's emotional response to sexual stimuli. If you are experiencing difficulties with your natural arousal response, it may be worth considering reducing or eliminating your porn use. Seeking the help of a therapist or other mental health professional can also be beneficial in addressing these issues and restoring your natural arousal response.

In my office when I'm talking with someone about this, I can tell when it's a serious issue. In my opinion, negative conditioning is the major downside of porn, but there are other issues to consider as well. It can also inhibit someone from being able to connect on a deep or spiritual level with his partner. As I'm sure you are aware, practically every major religion draws a "stop here" line in front of this type of behavior, and there are no doubt good reasons for doing so.

In the depths of desire's grip, I dwell,
A force unseen, a seductive spell.
I'm hidden in shadows, yet in plain sight,
A whispered secret, a silent fight.
As many are lured into my snare,
They yearn for escape, gasping for air.
A vicious cycle, a constant chase,
A battle with self, to find their grace.
What am I, that binds and breaks,
Leaving a trail of shattered fates?
Find your strength and set me free,
To claim your life and liberty.

The Five Motivations

Porn has a powerful pull in men's lives and attracts individuals for various reasons. If you want to get to the underlying issues that motivate some to return to porn again and again, you must explore the five key motivations that drive people to consume pornographic content: boredom, adrenaline-seeking, emotional regulation, alternative sexual activity, and manipulation. Understanding these motivations is crucial in addressing the challenges associated with excessive pornography use and in helping individuals find healthier coping mechanisms.

1. Boredom

Boredom is one of the primary reasons people turn to pornography. In today's fast-paced and technology-driven world, individuals often seek instant gratification and stimulation to counter feelings of restlessness and monotony. Pornography offers easy access to visual and auditory stimuli, making it a go-to solution for combating boredom. However, this convenience can lead to excessive consumption and psychological addiction, causing significant problems in the long run.

2. Seeking Adrenaline

Another motivation for using pornography is the pursuit of an adrenaline rush. The release of dopamine, a neurotransmitter associated with pleasure and reward, can create a sense of excitement and satisfaction. This adrenaline-seeking behavior can be particularly appealing for individuals who crave intense sensations or who struggle to find excitement in their daily lives. Pornography can provide a temporary high, but the constant pursuit of arousal can lead to compulsive consumption and addiction.

3. Emotional Regulation

Individuals struggling with emotional regulation may turn to pornography as a coping mechanism. By offering an escape from negative emotions and distressing situations, pornography can provide a sense of comfort and control. The consumption of explicit content can provide temporary relief from such negative emotions as stress, anxiety, and loneliness. By offering an escape from emotional turmoil, pornography becomes a powerful coping mechanism for those who have been unable to find healthier ways to manage their feelings. However, relying on pornography for emotional regulation can further complicate one's emotional struggles.

4. Alternative Sexual Experiences

Pornography can serve as an alternative for those who seek sexual experiences that are unavailable or unattainable in their real lives. The vast array of adult content available online caters to diverse tastes and preferences, allowing individuals to explore their fantasies and desires without judgment. For some, pornography provides a safe space to engage with their sexual interests when they cannot find a compatible partner or fulfill certain fantasies with their existing partners. As a result, the ability to access a wide range of sexual experiences through pornography can be a compelling reason for its consumption.

5. Manipulation

Lastly, some individuals may turn to pornography as a form of pathogenic manipulation or rebellion against what they perceive as wrongs in their lives. This is a particularly self-destructive motivation. For some men, porn use is an act of defiance or a passive-aggressive technique used to rail against their situations, partners, or spouses. Imagine someone saying, "I give you everything else in my life, but this is mine."

To summarize, the alluring appeal of porn can be attributed to several factors, including boredom, adrenaline-seeking, emotional regulation, alternative sexual experiences, and manipulation. Understanding these reasons is critical in addressing the complex relationship individuals have with pornography and developing healthier and more constructive ways of managing their desires and emotions. While pornography may offer temporary relief and excitement, it is essential to recognize the potential risks associated with excessive consumption and to strive for balance in all aspects of life.

How to Break Free

To become your best sexual self you must overcome your desire to use porn and recondition your body's arousal mechanism to respond to the stimuli present in a normal sexual encounter.

Breaking free from the power and allure of porn is a challenging process that requires both a behavioral and insight-oriented approach. There are many ways to seek help if porn is a problem for you. Below, I've provided a simple step-by-step guide that can assist you in breaking free from its grip:

Recognize the problem: The first step towards breaking free from porn is to recognize that it is a problem. Acknowledge that porn consumption is having a negative impact on your life, your relationships, and your well-being. Take responsibility. Own it. Do not blame others. Be strong—you can do it. You can break free. If your body has become conditioned by porn, it will of course take time and effort, but you can recondition your body.

Identify triggers: Identify the triggers that lead to your use of porn. Triggers can be different for different people. What triggers you? A stressful situation? Boredom? Loneliness? Identify what brings on you the urge to wander down the porn rabbit-hole. Once you see what the trigger, or the triggers are, you will never unsee them again.

Develop healthy coping mechanisms: Develop healthy ways to cope with and overcome the triggers. For instance, you could exercise, meditate, read, play a video game, watch a TV show or YouTube video, or you could socialize instead of using porn.

Set boundaries: Set boundaries around porn. For instance, you can limit your access to devices or websites that enable porn consumption. There are site blockers, keyloggers, apps, and parental controls options that can assist you in the early stages of maintaining the boundaries you have set for yourself.

Seek support: Seek support from friends, family, a coach, an accountability partner or a therapist. Having a supportive network can help you stay motivated and keep you on track.

Practice self-compassion: Practice self-compassion. Forgive yourself for past mistakes. Breaking free from porn is a process, and it's okay to stumble along the way. Setbacks could easily happen, but if and when one does, don't let it derail you. You're not perfect—no one is. If you stumble, take a moment, stop, reflect, and start again.

Engage in self-reflection: Take time in self-reflection to gain insight into the underlying reasons for your porn use. For example, you might discover that it's rooted in childhood trauma, low self-esteem, fear of attachment to others, or perhaps it's one of the five motivations mentioned above.

Challenge negative thoughts: Challenge negative thoughts and beliefs that perpetuate porn use. For instance, you might believe that porn is harmless. Or maybe you think you're addicted and cannot overcome your addiction. But you can. Others have done it and so can you. Do not give porn more power that it deserves.

Replace negative habits with positive habits: Replace negative habits with positive ones. For instance, if using porn is something you do when you're bored, find other activities that bring you joy and fulfillment.

Celebrate progress: Celebrate your progress and successes, no matter how small they may seem. Breaking free from porn is a significant achievement, and you should be proud of yourself for taking steps towards a healthier and happier life.

Become Your Best Sexual Self

It's important to face reality head on if you are to become your best sexual self, and that means the secret revealed in this chapter—*Porn Conditions You*—is one to take seriously. If what you have read caused you to realize that your porn use may have negatively conditioned you, I hope you will follow the steps listed above. It will take time and effort, and it may even be possible that the help of a therapist will be required. Nevertheless, I can assure you, it will be well worth doing whatever it takes.

> I am something that can hold you tight,
> And steal your joy day and night.
> I'm not a chain, but you can't break free,
> You'll feel trapped, no matter where you'll be.
> Many try to escape my grasp,
> But find it hard, as I will clasp,
> Onto their thoughts, their time, their soul,
> And make them feel they have no control.
> Yet, there is a way to find release,
> And make the grip of me decrease.
> It starts with admitting that I'm there,

Secrets of Men

And seeking help from those who care.
Through effort, time, and grace, you'll see,
That you can find your way to be free.
From the burden that has held you down,
And joy and peace in you will abound.
So tell me, what am I? Freedom from Porn

Chapter Seven: Own Your Masculinity

The secret revealed in this chapter is based on the reality that to be your best sexual self you must be and remain attractive and appealing to your significant other. You want to turn her on as often today as you did back at the beginning of your relationship, right? Isn't that necessary in order to have and enjoy a healthy relationship and a great sex life? You bet it is, and one way to ensure that is to maintain your masculine identity. That being the case, the secret revealed in this chapter, succinctly put:

Own Your Masculinity

Not only is projecting masculinity important for you to remain attractive to your sexual partner, as will be discussed, but it also bolsters your ability to create intimacy that will ensure an ongoing healthy and fulfilling relationship.

Paul and Tonya Revisited

Remember Paul and Tonya from a few chapters back? When they first met, the sexual chemistry between them was intense, but by the time Paul came to see me, things weren't going well. Sex for Paul and Tonya had become routine, boring, and unsatisfying. They knew it was happening but couldn't find a way to remedy the situation. Their emotional connection had waned, and they no longer communicated as they once did. It was clear that something needed to be done to turn the situation around.

Paul in particular was concerned. He instinctively understood where things could lead—but didn't know why or how to fix it. I suspect you recall that when it came to sex, he had slipped into a performance mindset, which is a common trap. His fears became his reality because, "where the mind goes the body follows." So together Paul and I developed a plan to get things back on track, and it worked.

In addition to the need to jettison his performance mentality, another issue had to be addressed and resolved before their relationship would return to full bloom. It had to do with expressions of intimacy in the relationship and how Paul viewed himself. Over time, counseling revealed that Paul's sense of self had diminished during the years he and Tonya had been together. It was clear that to a significant degree, he had lost his sense of self because he had not maintained his own masculine identity. This happens often to men who focus the majority of their time and energy on a relationship while neglecting his own interests. This was not only detrimental to Paul, but it was also harming his relationship with Tonya. I have found that it's essential for men to maintain their masculine identity in order to ensure an ongoing healthy and fulfilling, long-term relationship. Maintaining your masculinity helps you project confidence, and you and I know that confidence is one of the most important components of attraction. Consider what these experts have to say about this:

"In a healthy relationship, both partners should feel safe, secure, and respected. For many men, part of feeling secure is maintaining their sense of masculinity. This doesn't mean that a man has to be overly aggressive or dominating, but rather that he feels confident in himself and his ability to provide for and protect his partner."

—Dr. John Gray

"Maintaining masculinity in a relationship is about being true to yourself and your values. It's not about being controlling or dominating, but rather about being a strong, confident partner who can provide emotional and physical support."

—Mark Manson

"Masculinity in a relationship is important because it allows for a certain balance of power dynamics that can help sustain long-term intimacy. Men need to be able to assert themselves as protectors and providers, while also being emotionally available and supportive of their partners."

—Dr. Alexandra Solomon

"Maintaining your masculinity in a relationship means being confident in who you are as a man and not compromising your values or beliefs. It's about being strong and assertive, while also being respectful and loving towards your partner."

—Patrick Banks

"Being masculine in a relationship is not about dominating your partner or being controlling. It's about taking responsibility for your own actions and being a strong support for your partner. It's about being a leader, but also knowing when to listen and be vulnerable."

—Michael Jordan

"Men need to maintain their masculinity in relationships because it's a crucial part of their identity. When they feel like they're losing that sense of self, they can become depressed, anxious, or even physically ill."

—Dr. Robert Glover

As stated above, a diminished sense of self and masculinity has a number of potential downsides, which include depression and inability to perform at a high level sexually. It can also inhibit the ability to initiate activities that foster intimacy with a partner. So the question is, how do you get it back? Here are some actions you can take that worked for Paul:

Set boundaries: Establish boundaries with your partner and make sure that she respects them. This includes boundaries around your time, personal space, and what you're willing to compromise on.

Pursue your own interests: Continue to do the things that you enjoy and pursue your own hobbies and interests. Don't give them up just because you're in a relationship.

Spend time with male friends: Maintaining close relationships with male friends outside of the relationship can help you maintain a sense of self.

Communicate your needs: It's important to communicate your needs and desires to your partner. Don't be afraid to speak up and advocate for yourself. Men can easily lose themselves when they are silently providing for the relationship.

Spend time apart: It's healthy to spend time apart from your partner and have some independence. This will give you the opportunity to maintain your own identity and have a life outside of the relationship. No, you do not have to stay in constant contact with your partner throughout the day.

Stay true to yourself: It's important to stay true to your values and beliefs. Don't compromise them just to make your partner happy. This includes your sexual needs and desires.

Have a support system: It's important to have a support system outside of your relationship. This includes friends, family, and other people who can provide you with emotional support and advice when needed.

Practice self-care: Take care of yourself physically, emotionally, and mentally. This includes getting enough sleep, exercise, taking time for self-reflection, and staying involved in activities that make you happy.

Be aware of red flags: Pay attention to any red flags in your relationship that may be indicative of your partner trying to control or manipulate you. If you notice any, address them immediately.

Keep yourself fit: Keeping yourself fit and groomed can make you more attractive to your partner. Dressing nicely and taking care of your hygiene is a must.

Reestablishing Intimacy

Recapturing and maintaining your masculine identity will also enable you to establish and enjoy a strong bond of intimacy with your partner more readily. Ongoing intimacy is extremely important and can take many different forms. Here are some to consider perusing in order to foster and maintain a more deeply fulfilling relationship:

Physical intimacy: Physical intimacy involves physical touch and closeness between partners, such as hugging, kissing, holding hands, cuddling, and sexual encounters.

Emotional intimacy: Emotional intimacy involves sharing thoughts, feelings, and emotions with a partner. This can include deep conversations, sharing secrets, and being vulnerable with each other.

Intellectual intimacy: Intellectual intimacy involves sharing ideas and intellectual interests with a partner. This can include discussing books, movies, or current events, or engaging in activities that stimulate the mind.

Spiritual intimacy: Spiritual intimacy involves sharing spiritual beliefs and practices with a partner. This can include attending religious services together, practicing meditation or yoga, or exploring spiritual ideas and concepts.

Experiential intimacy: Experiential intimacy involves sharing experiences and creating memories together as a couple. This can include traveling together, trying new activities or hobbies, or simply enjoying each other's company in everyday activities.

Recreational intimacy: Recreational intimacy involves engaging in activities or hobbies together that bring joy and fun to the relationship. This can include playing sports together, going to concerts or events, or simply watching a favorite TV show or movie.

Creative intimacy: Creative intimacy involves engaging in creative activities together, such as writing, painting, or cooking. This can foster a sense of connection and collaboration between partners, as well as a shared sense of accomplishment and satisfaction.

The Three Types of Intimacy That Involve Touch

When I counsel and teach regarding intimacy within a relationship, I focus on three types of intimacies that involve touch: Emotional, Sensual, and Sexual. I'll go into some detail about each of them since they are perhaps the most important when it comes to building and maintaining a close relationship. This is probably one of the areas that couples can really miss the most. However, with a few simple adjustments, you can significantly help your relationship.

When you think about emotional intimacy, you're considering the different ways to feel loved by sharing thoughts, feelings, and emotions with a partner. This can include deep conversations, sharing secrets, and being vulnerable with each other. There is touch that accompanies emotional intimacy. Think of hugs, kisses on the cheek before you leave for work, and cuddling on the couch while watching a show. These actions communicate affection, affirmation, warmth and love through touch, and they do so at a high level that cannot be attained in any other way. You might say, they are "beyond words" in that touch has a way of communicating deep feelings that words cannot.

Most couples engage in some capacity of emotional intimacy. It's common in most relationships along with the examples of touch mentioned above. The difficulty is that most couples try to jump from emotional intimacy to sexual intimacy. That usually doesn't go very well. Imagine, a guy hugs his girl and then tries to jump into something sexual with her. Like I said, it doesn't go very well.

When couples engage in sexual intimacy, they allow themselves to become vulnerable, and they give themselves to one other completely as they move toward pleasure and an orgasmic experience. It's wild, it's fun, and it can be very enriching. That's what we all want to experience!

However, there is a third intimacy that involves touch: Sensual Intimacy. One way to think of *sensual* intimacy is that it exists somewhere between emotional intimacy and sexual intimacy. Sensual intimacy communicates that you are into her and that you love her. It happens through actions such as a caress, or maybe walking up behind her, wrapping your arms around her, softly cupping her breasts and telling her how much you miss her and love her. It can be the time on the couch, watching TV, when she reaches over to caress your member. It can be a deep, long kiss that feels great and is wonderful to experience all to itself. It's sensual, not sexual. There is a difference. With sensual intimacy, the couple is simply communicating their physical attraction to one another that is playful, erotic, and fun.

I believe when the couple is freely able to express their physical attraction to each other without pressure to perform sexually, they are activating a high level of connectedness.

Have you ever wondered why she doesn't act flirty and erotic around you? You may not like the answer. The main reason couples do not engage in sensual intimacy in their relationship is because men misinterpret being sensual as sexual foreplay. Don't believe me? Okay, Let's say she begins to touch him playfully and he becomes erect. Then he communicates to her either, by word or action, "You got this started, now you need to finish it." She wasn't touching him to start something. She was touching him because she knew that he enjoyed it. But now that he's aroused, he applies pressure to her to finish the job. She knows that if she doesn't finish the job, he is going to pout, call her out, get upset, keep pressing her to go further. Does any of this sound familiar? What lesson do you think she learns from this? Perhaps she begins to say to herself, "It's not worth the trouble." She stops being playful, stops being sensual because of how he reacts to being aroused.

This dynamic is played out on my therapy couch every single week. Let goes something like this, I'm talking with a couple about what they sensually and sexually enjoy doing with each other, and she will say, "I like long, deep kisses."

He looks over at her and says, "No you don't."

She replies, "Yes I do."

"So why don't we do it more often," he said.

"Because I know what's coming next. If I don't want to finish you off, you get upset with me."

Here's what probably happened. Somewhere when the relationship was young, she kissed him deeply, and he thought that she was initiating sex. He probably got an erection and wanted to use it. However, the long, deep kiss was all she wanted at the time. That's when he would give her so much crap for leaving him with an erection. He may have even pouted the rest of the night. He may have gotten upset with her, hounded her for the rest of the night. She quickly learned a lesson. After that, she understood that giving him a long, deep kiss would come with a consequence.

But please remember, she wasn't trying to pissed him off. She wasn't trying to tease him, she was just being sensual with him. Whatever the case may have been, it didn't take long for her to learn: "Don't do it. It's not worth it." In that moment, she began to shut down her sensual size. She realized that if she turned him down, she likely would have a price to pay. He'd pout, or maybe he'd make fun of her, call her names, all of which served to shut down any expressions of sensual intimacy going forward.

The unfortunate consequences were two fold: 1) her sensual self was shut down; 2) he wondered why she was no longer as affectionate as she once was.

Along with emotional intimacy and sexual intimacy, it's important also to have a strong, ongoing flow of sensual intimacy, and for that to happen, sensual intimacy has to be able to exist by itself. Men have to understand that sensual intimacy on her part doesn't always lead to sex. One of the best lessons men can learn in their masculinity is that they can be turned on—have an erection—and do not have to get a release right then.

When men learn that they can be in a sensual intimate moment with their partner, they will experience more sensual intimacy flowing within the relationship more freely. Which will allow for anticipation to build for the next time they are together with their partner sexually. They simply need to learn to let sensual intimacy stand on its own.

I tell guys, comically of course, "You need to learn to run with a hard on." What I'm hoping to communicate is that it's okay to go through the day sexually aroused without having to get a release every time you're hard. Men need to be able to let their partners be their sensual, sexual selves without suffering any consequences.

When I'm working with couples on this issue, they often have an "Ah-ha!" moment. This happened with Paul and Tonya, and the result was that Paul began to allow Tonya's sensuality to develop again. They told me about an encounter they had in the kitchen one Saturday afternoon. They were enjoying a deep kiss. He felt his erection forming. He heard Tonya begin to breathe harder realizing she was getting turned on. Then he stepped away and simply said, "Where would you like to go to dinner tonight?" She loved it!

Secrets of Men

In summary, once Paul began allowing sensual intimacy to have a place in their relationship, Tonya responded, and she kept it going. One night he was lying on the coach, and she came over and began to give him a blowjob—but didn't finish him off. Paul was in a much better headspace to simply enjoy the moment with her without pressuring her to continue. His new mindset communicated so much affection and appreciation to her, and in the process, he was able to reignite her sensual self. Now they can sit on the sofa, and he can play with her, and she with him while they are watching a show. They feel less pressure to perform. They simply enjoy the intimacy.

To take this point to the apex of sensuality, one night when they were in bed, she turned to him and said, "Will you enter me? Just be inside me—nothing more?"

She just wanted to feel him there, and so he did enter her, and simply fell asleep holding each other. Of course, Paul's erection went down as he drifted off to sleep.

Tonya later stated that that experience was one of the most fulfilling nights she ever had—feeling so connected with him.

So, I know what you're saying to yourself, first, "That's not possible!" Second, "How am I supposed to tell if she just wants something sensual or something more? I tell couples they need to be able to communicate to one another when it's just play and when it's foreplay. Over time, with practice, the couple develops something of a "sixth sense" about it. They learn to read each other that well. Believe me, you will know when she wants more.

When a couple starts wrestling with this concept, I will often tell them just use the word "play" to mean that what's happening is just something sensual. For example, "Do you mind if I just play with you?" Use a word or two to communicate that this is as far as it's going to go.

This lesson is one of the hardest for men to learn, but once they grasp it, it can revolutionize their sexual lives. Try it.

In Summary

The secret I hope I have communicated in this chapter is based on the reality that to be your best sexual self you must maintain your masculinity by understanding the role of intimacy; especially sensual intimacy in the relationship. This is how you will remain attractive and appealing to your significant other. So please keep this chapter's secret in mind:

Own Your Masculinity

Not only will projecting your masculinity be important in order to remain attractive to your significant other, it will also bolster your ability to create intimacy that will ensure an ongoing healthy and fulfilling relationship.

Chapter Eight: Evoke your Primal Sexual Energy

Throughout this book, you have read about aspects of masculinity, including how to achieve mastery. You've read about alpha wolves, rhymes and riddles, and paths that you can take toward becoming your best sexual self. The seventh and final secret is the icing on the cake:

Evoke Your Primal Sexual Energy

To help you do so, I would like to introduce you to a kreature that perhaps dwells within the soul of every male human being—Pan.

Rest assured, I do not mean the Peter Pan character of Disney and Captain Hook—not at all. I'm thinking more of the Pan that legend says inhabited the earth when everything was young, even before the Greek gods took up residence on Mount Olympus. That's right, before there was Zeus, Apollo, or even the goddess Aphrodite, there was Pan. Half-goat, half-man—he was unabashed masculinity incarnate, a god of the forest and of all things wild, including sex and passion.

The Legend of Pan

When the world was still young and the veil between the earthly realm and the divine realm was thin, there was a kreature known as Pan. He was a being of great power, with the ability to move between worlds and to speak with spirits that dwelt primarily on the other side.

Pan was known as the kreature of the wild, the forests, and the untamed places of the earth. His voice and his flute could be heard echoing throughout the valleys and the mountains.

Pan was kreature of a primal nature—a primordial being. He embodied the essence of male sexuality, and his power over the physical realm was a result of this masculine energy. His presence could be felt in the heat of passion and the wild abandonment of the flesh. Pan also represented transformation. Transformation of the wild and of man's psyche.

Legend has it that Pan's lower half was that of a goat, symbolizing his connection to the earth and the animalistic nature of his humanity. His horns represented his power and his ability to channel the primal energy of the universe.

Those who understood the power of the male sexual essence sought Pan in secret. Rituals to Pan often were held in secluded places, deep in the heart of the forest or on the banks of a hidden stream. There his followers would evoke his name and offer themselves up to his power. For those initiated into the mysteries of Pan, his energy was transformative. It was said that his touch and his words brought forth enormous wisdom, passion, sensuality, and love.

But Pan was an erratic kreature, and if his power was misused, the result could be dangerous. Those who sought to harness his energy without proper respect and understanding risked being consumed by his primal nature and lost forever in the wild, untamed regions of the earth.

In the end, as the world grew more and more civilized, the search for Pan faded. But his legend lives on, a reminder of the power of the male sexual essence and the primal nature of humanity that lies just beneath the surface of our twenty-first century, civilized veneer.

The Godgame

Allow me to tell one last story, please. John Fowles' 1965 novel, *The Magus,* is a gripping tale of self-discovery, deception, and psychological manipulation. Set against the backdrop of the picturesque Greek island of Phraxos, the novel follows the journey of Nicholas Urfe, a young Englishman who is hired as a teacher at an all-boys school. The narrative explores the intricacies of human relationships and the quest for self-understanding through a series of mind-bending twists and turns. At its core, *The Magus* is an exploration of the role of personal responsibility in determining one's own destiny, as exemplified by the transformation of its protagonist, Nicholas Urfe.

The story begins with Nicholas feeling disillusioned with his life in England, prompting him to seek a fresh start on the idyllic island of Phraxos. This escape is in part an attempt to distance himself from a failed love affair with a woman named Alison. Upon arriving at the island, Nicholas is quickly captivated by the mysterious figure of Maurice Conchis, a wealthy recluse living in a nearby villa. Conchis claims to be a former psychiatrist and a student of the human mind, but his true intentions remain elusive.

Secrets of Men

As Nicholas becomes increasingly fascinated with Conchis, he is drawn into a series of elaborate psychological games and manipulations. "The Magus," which is the singular form of magi, which means "magicians" in Persian, is a reference to Conchis' ability to wield power over the minds of others. These manipulations, referred to as the "godgame," involve elaborate masquerades and staged events, designed to confuse, enlighten, and ultimately provoke self-discovery in the participant. As the novel unfolds, Nicholas finds himself at the center of these mind games, with the lines between reality and illusion becoming increasingly blurred.

The Magus is a labyrinthine journey through the depths of the human psyche. Throughout the novel, Nicholas is forced to confront the consequences of his actions, both in his past and in his current interactions with Conchis and the other characters. As the godgame progresses, Nicholas must navigate a series of moral dilemmas and ethical quandaries, grappling with the ramifications of his choices on both himself and those around him.

One prominent symbol within the story is that of the Greek god Pan, who serves as a representation of the primal, untamed aspects of human nature and the power of transformation.

Pan is the god of shepherds, flocks, and wild, untamed nature in Greek mythology. Being half-human, half-goat, Pan embodies the dual nature of man as both rational and irrational, civilized and wild. This dualism is central to the themes of *The Magus* and plays a significant role in Nicholas Urfe's psychological journey.

Secrets of Men

Throughout the novel, the presence of Pan can be felt in various ways. For instance, the island of Phraxos, where much of the story takes place, is characterized by its wild, untamed landscape, which serves as a physical manifestation of Pan's influence. Pan serves as a symbol of the transformative power that lies at the heart of *The Magus*. As the god of nature and transformation, Pan represents the potential for change and growth inherent in every individual. In the novel, this potential is embodied by the psychological metamorphosis that Nicholas undergoes as he participates in the godgame orchestrated by Maurice Conchis.

One particular powerful scene featuring the Dionysian ritual involving the worship of Pan is a pivotal moment in the story, as it represents a key turning point in Nicholas Urfe's psychological journey. This mysterious and enigmatic encounter occurs when Nicholas is led deep into the forest on the island of Phraxos by one of the elusive female characters, Lily.

The scene is set against the backdrop of a moonlit night, with the natural beauty of the forest enhancing the sense of otherworldliness and mystique. As Nicholas follows Lily deeper into the woods, they come upon a clearing where a group of people is gathered, seemingly in the throes of a primal, ecstatic celebration.

The participants, adorned in goat skins and other animalistic costumes, are engaged in a wild, uninhibited dance. As the ritual unfolds, Nicholas becomes aware that the worshipers are paying homage to the ancient Greek god Pan, whose presence can be felt throughout the novel in various forms and symbols.

The Dionysian ritual itself is characterized by its chaotic, liberating energy, as the worshipers revel in their primal instincts and desires. The celebration appears to be a means of connecting with the untamed, irrational aspects of human nature, which are often suppressed in the name of civilization and order. The scene is marked by a sense of transcendence, as the participants temporarily cast off the constraints of society and embrace their wild, animalistic selves.

By exposing Nicholas to this primal, ecstatic celebration, Fowles invites readers to question their understanding of the boundaries between rationality and irrationality, civilization and savageness, and the role these dualities play in the quest for self-discovery and personal growth.

As Nicholas becomes more deeply immersed in the godgame, the symbolism of Pan continues to shape his understanding of personal responsibility. The god's dual nature, as both a source of chaos and an agent of transformation, mirrors Nicholas' own journey towards self-discovery and self-acceptance. By engaging with the untamed aspects of his own psyche, Nicholas is able to confront the moral dilemmas and ethical quandaries that arise throughout the story, ultimately recognizing the importance of personal responsibility in shaping his own destiny.

In essence, the symbolism of Pan in *The Magus* serves as a catalyst for Nicholas Urfe's confrontation with his own responsibilities and the complexities of human nature.

In the world of today, the thought of seeking Pan and the male sexual essence that he represents may seem absolutely absurd. Nevertheless, I believe that there's still room in this world for the chaotic and transformative power that the Pan figure represents. May I invite you to imagine that the *Secrets of Men* you have discovered in this book were actually passed down from man to man for centuries, perhaps having originated with Pan himself—the ultimate masculine half human, half animal creature? His secrets are still important today—no, make that *essential* today—essential to know and practice in order to become your very best sexual self. As we see in Fowles' character Nicholas, the deepest delves of self-exploration reveal a combination of passionate energy and personal responsibility. That is what I call your best sexual self. With that in mind, I urge you to embrace all the secrets, including this final one:

Evoke Your Primal Sexual Energy

Men, I urge you to call up other men, get together, and let them know what you now know. I also want to encourage you to summon the courage to live more deeply in your masculinity and desires. I sincerely want you to be your best sexual self.

The Secrets of Men

Here they are. Please take them to heart:

1. The first secret we explored centered on knowing yourself sexually: "Embrace Your Erotic

Profile." Remember the exercises in Chapter Two? If you haven't taken advantage of them, I urge you to do so. Knowing your personal erotic profile is basic to becoming your best sexual self.

2. In Chapter Three we explored the secret, "Your Sexual Best Is Built." You see, an ongoing sexual relationship that's consistently fulfilling takes effort to achieve—it has to be created and fostered. Assuming that's what you want, and I'll bet it is, it's going to require work to build an environment in which sensual desire can flourish. Chapter Three gave you some tools.

3. "Confidence Is Sexy" was the secret revealed in Chapter Four. It's also true that a lack of confidence can lead to issues that can keep you forever from becoming your best sexual self. This chapter suggested ways to acquire confidence, or if you have it already, how to bolster what you already have.

4. The secret of Chapter Five is that to become your best sexual self, you must "Face Sexual Shame." If shame is an issue for you, this is a secret to take very seriously. You must face that shame, see where it came from, overcome it, and put it behind you.

5. The secret of Chapter Six is that to become your best sexual self, you must realize "Porn Conditions You." This means you must over-

come your desire to use porn and then reconditioning your body's arousal mechanism to respond to the stimuli present in a normal sexual encounter. It will take time and effort. It may even be possible that the help of a therapist will be required, but I assure you, it will be well worth your effort.

6. The secret of Chapter Seven was stated as, "Own Your Masculinity." Projecting masculinity is one key to remaining attractive to your sexual partner as well as what helps make it possible for you to create intimacy that ensures an ongoing healthy and fulfilling relationship. Steps were revealed you can take to regain or enhance your masculine side as were various ways to establish and maintain a strong bond of intimacy with your significant other. Doing so will greatly enhance your relationship sexually and in other ways as well.

7. And finally, the secret of Chapter Eight was, "Evoke Your Primal Sexual Energy." You are a man, the descendant of a long line of men that goes back to primordial. Imagine the *Secrets of Men* were handed down from him. Embrace his chaotic, passionate energy as well as personal responsibility as you immerse yourself into your sexual best.

Secrets of Men

Thank you for taking this journey with me. As the saying goes, "life is short." There's no reason to spend it not being your very best sexual self. Great sex and a great sexual relationship can make the difference between a boring life and one filled with excitement, pleasure and fulfillment. I've given you the tools that I believe you can use to achieve just that. Now it is up to you. Consider your completion of this book as the beginning of a conversation. Take the opportunities to connect with others who understand that sex is important and that a great sex life must be built. Watch for additional *Secrets of Men* to reveal themselves to you. For example, did you know that there is a unique pressure point called the "golden button" that when pressed at the height of your arousal, your ejaculate will recess back into your shaft allowing you to last a lot longer during sex? Did you know there are ways to maintain your erection after you ejaculated? The masters of ejaculatory control can maintain their erections long after climax and even climax multiple times in one sexual encounter. Creating a fulfilling and fun sexual life for yourself is not all that complicated, you simply have to begin with intention. You simply have to devote the time and the energy and go on the journey set forth in this book. Do that and it surely will happen.

"Stay Hard My Friends." – Dr. Nic

About the Author

Nicholas A. Natale, Ph.D., is a Licensed Professional Counselor, Certified Sex Therapist (AASECT), and Certified Hypnotherapist who has received advanced training in the areas of marriage therapy, sex therapy, problematic sexual behavior, depressive disorders, and leadership development. He currently maintains a private  practice in Columbia, South Carolina as well as a coaching practice reaching individuals around the world.

Dr. Nic is passionate about helping people embrace the strength within. As a counselor, hypnotist, traveler, and spiritualist, he draws out the best in others. His inner alchemy work also addresses the shadow side many people experience. Assisting individuals in reaching new levels of healthy relationships and restoring pieces of the fragmented self. Restoring, Building, Mastering, Healing.

Dr. Nic has spoken in conferences in the US and internationally, including Portugal, India, Mexico, and Pakistan. He has addressed business professionals, college faculties, church leaders, humanitarian workers, and families on the subjects of "Strengthening Marriages," "Intimacy in the Field," "Disaster Relief Debriefing," "Depression among Leaders," "Spiritual Abuse," and many others.

You can reach Dr. Nic through his website: www.nicnatale.com

Addendum: Hypnotic Scripts

Hypnotic scripts are powerful tools that can be used to help people achieve their desired outcomes by tapping into the subconscious mind. Whether you are a professional hypnotist, or someone interested in self-hypnosis, these scripts can be used to guide clients into a state of deep relaxation and focused attention. By using language and visualization techniques that are specifically designed to bypass the critical conscious mind and access the subconscious, these scripts can help you to achieve the intended goals explored within the *Secrets of Men*. It is also possible to overcome fears and limitations and create positive changes in your overall life. In this chapter, you will find hypnotic scripts similar to what I use while taking clients through their own discoveries. These are generic in style, however, so feel free to personalize them to your own purpose. Please feel free to use them in your own personal journey or to guide someone else towards personal transformation.

Use whatever induction process you are accustomed to and believe would be most effective for the subject. If you are exploring self-hypnosis, the following script to place you in a respective hypnotic state.

Self-hypnotic Induction
Find a quiet and comfortable place where you won't be disturbed for the next few minutes. Sit down or lie down in a

comfortable position. Follow the first few steps as presented and then add additional insights and visualizations from the other scripts.

Take a few deep breaths and allow your body to relax. Close your eyes and focus on your breath. Inhale deeply and exhale slowly. Let go of any tension in your body with each exhale.

Imagine a peaceful place where you feel completely relaxed and at ease. It could be a beach, a forest, or a peaceful meadow. Imagine yourself being there right now, surrounded by nature's beauty.

Visualize a spiral staircase in front of you that leads down to a deeper level of relaxation. With each step down, feel yourself becoming more and more relaxed. Countdown from 10 to 1 with each step you take.

Once you reach the bottom of the staircase, imagine a white light surrounding you. Feel the warmth and comfort of this light as it envelops you in its soothing energy.

Repeat the following affirmations to yourself: "I am calm and relaxed. I am in control of my thoughts and emotions. I am confident and focused. I am capable of achieving my goals." Or, include visualizations from the other scripts. Count from 1 to 5, and when you reach 5, open your eyes feeling refreshed and energized.

For Sexual Awakening

As you begin to relax, you may notice a heaviness in your eyelids, a softness in your breath, and a sense of calm spreading throughout your body. You may also become aware of my voice, which is here to guide you into a state of deep relaxation and suggestibility.

And as you continue to relax, you may become more and more aware of your breathing, feeling it slow and steady as your body sinks deeper into relaxation.

Now, I want you to imagine yourself in a peaceful place, somewhere you feel completely at ease and relaxed. Perhaps it's a beach, a forest, a mountain retreat, or a cozy cabin by a lake. Whatever that place may be, allow yourself to fully immerse in the sights, sounds, and feelings of that place. Go there now.

As you sink deeper into this state of relaxation, you may notice a gentle sensation spreading throughout your body, a sign that your subconscious mind is opening up to new possibilities and suggestions.

And in this state of heightened suggestibility, I want you to focus on your body, on your physical sensations, on your breath, and on your thoughts.

As you do so, you may become aware of any tensions, anxieties, or worries that are holding you back from enjoying a fulfilling and satisfying sex life. You may also become aware of any limiting beliefs, negative self-talk, or past experiences that are keeping you from experiencing pleasure and intimacy in the way you want to.

And as you become aware of these patterns and tendencies, I want you to remind yourself that they are simply habits, patterns of behavior that can be changed, transformed.

And now, I want you to imagine a bright light, a light that represents your deepest desires, your highest potential, and your truest self. This light is pure, loving, and healing, and it's here to guide you towards a state of sexual vitality, confidence, and erotic joy.

As you focus on this light, you may feel a warmth spreading throughout your body, a warmth that represents the healing power of your own mind and imagination.

And as you feel this warmth, I want you to repeat to yourself the following affirmations, knowing that they are true, valid, and full of power:

I am a healthy, vibrant, and sexually confident man

I am worthy of pleasure, intimacy, and connection
I trust my body to respond naturally and spontaneously to what arouses me

I let go of any past traumas, fears, or doubts that may be holding me back

I embrace my sexuality with joy, curiosity, and openness

I communicate my needs, desires, and boundaries with ease and confidence

I am capable of experiencing deep and meaningful connection with my partner(s)

And as you repeat these affirmations, you may notice a shift in your body, a sense of relaxation, ease, and pleasure. You may also notice a renewed sense of curiosity, playfulness, and spontaneity.

And in this state of heightened sexual awareness and openness, I want you to imagine yourself in a sexual situation, perhaps with a person or persons of your choice. Imagine yourself fully engaged, fully present, and fully responsive to the sensations and feelings of pleasure that arise.

And as you imagine this scene, I want you to notice the subtle shifts and changes in your body, the way your muscles relax and respond, the way your breath deepens and quickens, the way your mind becomes focused and alert.

And as you continue to focus on this scene, you may notice a powerful surge of sexual energy rising up within you, a sense of confidence, vitality, and pleasure that is completely natural and spontaneous.

And in this state of heightened sexual awareness and openness, I want you to imagine yourself overcoming any obstacles or challenges that may have previously held you back from experiencing pleasure and intimacy in the way you want to.

Perhaps you imagine yourself communicating your needs and desires with ease and confidence, or maybe you see yourself trying new positions, techniques, or sensations that enhance your pleasure.

Whatever you envision, allow yourself to fully embrace it, knowing that your mind and body are capable of experiencing pleasure, joy, and fulfillment in limitless ways.
And as you continue to focus on this scene, I want you to repeat to yourself the following affirmations, knowing that they are true, valid, and full of power:

I am a sexually confident and empowered man

I trust my body to respond naturally and spontaneously to what arouses me

I embrace my sexuality with joy, curiosity, and openness

I communicate my needs, desires, and boundaries with ease and confidence

I am capable of experiencing deep and meaningful connection with my partner(s)

I am worthy of pleasure, intimacy, and connection

And as you repeat these affirmations, allow yourself to fully embody them, feeling them resonate throughout your body and mind. Know that these affirmations are your truth, your reality, and your power.

And now, as we come to the end, I want you to allow yourself to slowly come back to your present surroundings, feeling refreshed, energized, and empowered.
And as you open your eyes, know that you have the power within you to transform your sexual experience, to overcome any obstacles or challenges, and to embrace your sexuality with joy, confidence, and openness.

Sexual Confidence

Start by getting into a comfortable position, either lying down or sitting in a comfortable chair. Take a few deep breaths and allow your body to relax. Imagine that with each breath you take, you are sinking deeper and deeper into a state of relaxation.

As you focus on your breathing, I want you to imagine a warm, soothing light flowing through your body. This light is the color of confidence and sexual power, and with each breath you take, it grows stronger and brighter. As the light continues to flow through your body, imagine that it is clearing away any doubts, fears or insecurities you may have about your sexual ability. Allow the light to wash over you, filling you with a sense of confidence and assurance.

Imagine that you are standing in front of a mirror. As you look at yourself, you see a powerful, confident man staring back at you. This man knows exactly what he wants and how to get it. He is in control, and he knows it.

As you continue to look at this confident man in the mirror, you start to feel the same sense of power and control within yourself. You realize that you too are a powerful, confident man, capable of anything you set your mind to.

As you continue to focus on your breathing, imagine that you are standing in a beautiful, luxurious bedroom. The room is softly lit, and there is a comfortable bed in the center. You feel calm and relaxed, and you know that you are in complete control. As you look around the room, you see a beautiful woman standing in front of you. She is smiling and welcoming, and you know that she wants you just as much as you want her. You feel a surge of confidence and power within you, and you know that you are fully capable of satisfying her every desire.

As you look into her eyes, you feel a deep connection and understanding between the two of you. You know that you are meant to be together, and that you will have an amazing, fulfilling sexual experience. As you move closer to her, you feel the warmth of her body against yours. You feel the power and strength of your own body, and you know that you can please her in every way possible. You feel a deep sense of satisfaction and pride as you both reach the peak of pleasure together.

As you come back to your present surroundings, take a deep breath and know that you are a confident, powerful man, fully capable of achieving your sexual desires. You are in complete control, and you know that you will have amazing sexual experiences in the future.

Remember this feeling of confidence and power and carry it with you always. You are a sexual force to be reckoned with, and you know it.

Building Your Sexual Self

As you sit comfortably and relax, I want you to focus your attention on your breath. Allow your breath to become deeper and more rhythmic, as you sink deeper and deeper into a state of relaxation.

As you continue to breathe, imagine a warm and soothing light beginning to surround your body. This light is a manifestation of your own sexual energy, and it is pulsing with a vibrant, powerful energy.

As you tune in to this energy, allow yourself to feel a deep sense of connection to your sexual self. Visualize yourself as a skilled and confident lover, able to give and receive pleasure with ease and grace.

As you bask in this feeling, notice how your body begins to respond. Perhaps you feel a surge of arousal, or a tingling sensation in your genitals. Whatever you feel, allow yourself to fully embrace it and explore it.

Now, I want you to visualize a room in your mind. This room represents your inner world, the place where your sexual energy resides. As you enter this room, notice the colors, shapes, and textures that surround you. Perhaps there are objects or symbols that feel significant to you.

As you explore this room, allow yourself to feel a sense of curiosity and wonder. Notice how your body responds as you touch different objects or interact with different elements of the room.

As you continue to explore, allow your mind to connect with your body in new and exciting ways. Feel the power of your own sexual energy pulsing through every cell of your body, awakening you to new levels of pleasure and fulfillment.

Now, as we bring this session to a close, allow yourself to carry this feeling of connection and empowerment with you into your daily life. Know that you have the power to build and cultivate your sexual self, and that you are capable of experiencing profound pleasure and intimacy.

When you are ready, you can open your eyes and return to the present moment, feeling refreshed, energized, and empowered.

Embrace Masculinity
Take a deep breath, and as you exhale, allow any tension to leave your body. Close your eyes and let yourself become completely calm and relaxed.

Now, imagine yourself standing tall and strong, with a deep sense of purpose and confidence. Visualize your body growing bigger and more powerful with each passing moment. Feel the strength and energy radiating from within you. See yourself as a powerful and confident man who is in control of his life.

As you continue to breathe deeply and calmly, allow yourself to embrace your natural masculinity. Feel the power of your inner warrior, the strength of your inner protector, and the wisdom of your inner guide. Allow yourself to tap into the energy and strength that come with being a man.

You are a man, and you are proud of who you are. You are not afraid to take charge, to speak your mind, and to stand up for what you believe in. You are confident in your abilities, and you know that you can handle anything that comes your way. You are proud of your masculinity and the qualities that come with it.

Think about the qualities that define masculinity to you. Maybe it's strength, courage, or assertiveness. Maybe it's intelligence, responsibility, or leadership. Whatever it is, allow yourself to fully embrace these qualities and let them become a part of you.

Embrace your masculinity now, and feel it filling every corner of your being. Feel the power and energy flowing through your veins, and the courage and strength that come with being a man. You are powerful, you are confident, and you are in control.

As you continue to breathe deeply and calmly, allow these feelings to become a part of you. Embrace your masculinity and let it guide you in all that you do. Allow yourself to feel strong and powerful, and to take charge of your life. You are a man, and you are proud of it. You are confident, you are strong, and you are in control.

Think about the ways in which you can express your masculinity in your daily life. Maybe it's by taking on a leadership role at work or in your community. Maybe it's by pursuing your passions with courage and determination. Maybe it's by standing up for what you believe in, even in the face of opposition.

Whatever it is, allow yourself to fully embrace your masculinity and let it guide you towards your goals. Remember that being a man is not just about physical strength or assertiveness, but also about compassion, empathy, and respect for others.

Take one final deep breath, and as you exhale, allow yourself to slowly come back to the present moment. Open your eyes, and feel the power and strength of your masculinity with you, ready to tackle anything that comes your way. Remember that you are a powerful and confident man who is in control of his life. Embrace your masculinity and let it guide you towards a fulfilling and rewarding life.

Unlocking Erotic Potential
Before we begin, it's important to note that hypnosis is a tool to help you access your innermost thoughts and desires. It can assist you in unlocking your erotic potential, but the true work comes from within yourself. If at any point during this session you feel uncomfortable or want to stop, you can easily do so by simply opening your eyes.

Let's begin. I want you to find a comfortable position, whether that be sitting or lying down, and just allow yourself to relax. Take a deep breath in, hold it for a moment, and slowly release it. Feel your body sinking into the surface beneath you as you exhale.

As you continue to breathe deeply and slowly, I want you to focus on the sound of my voice. Imagine that every word I say is a soothing wave washing over you, calming your mind and body. Let all of your thoughts drift away, and just allow yourself to be fully present in this moment.

I want you to visualize yourself standing in front of a mirror. Take a moment to observe yourself - your features, your physique, your expressions. Notice how each part of your body is connected, and how it moves in harmony with the others.

As you look into the mirror, you realize that you are surrounded by an aura of energy. This energy is your erotic potential - the passion and desire that lies within you, waiting to be unleashed.

With each passing moment, you feel this energy growing stronger and more intense. It starts as a gentle hum, but soon becomes a roaring flame, consuming your body and mind. You are consumed by a deep, burning desire to explore your own sensuality and pleasure.

As you continue to gaze into the mirror, you begin to notice certain parts of your body becoming more sensitive and responsive to your touch. You realize that your erotic potential is not just a feeling, but a physical sensation as well.

I want you to focus on the parts of your body that are most sensitive and responsive to your touch. It could be your lips, your neck, your chest, or any other area that feels particularly erotic to you. Imagine that each touch sends a powerful wave of pleasure coursing through your body.

As you continue to explore your own sensuality, you become more and more aware of the infinite possibilities that lie within you. You realize that you are capable of experiencing pleasure beyond your wildest dreams, and that your erotic potential is limitless.

Now, I want you to repeat these affirmations to yourself:

I am in touch with my own sensuality and desire.

I am capable of experiencing pleasure beyond my wildest dreams.

My erotic potential is limitless.

Allow these affirmations to sink deep into your subconscious mind, so that you can access them whenever you need to. Take a deep breath in, and slowly exhale.

As you continue to focus on your own sensuality and desire, you may begin to notice certain sensations in your body. Perhaps you feel a warmth spreading through your chest or a tingling in your fingertips. These physical sen-

Secrets of Men

sations are a sign that you are fully connected with your own erotic potential.

I want you to imagine a scenario in which you are fully embracing your sensuality and desire. Perhaps you are in a romantic setting with a partner, or maybe you are simply exploring your own body in private. Whatever the scenario may be, I want you to fully immerse yourself in the experience, letting your imagination run wild.

As you continue to visualize this scenario, you may notice that your body is responding in ways that you didn't expect. Your breath may become more shallow and rapid, and your heart may begin to race. These are all signs that you are tapping into your deepest desires and unlocking your full erotic potential.

I want you to focus on the pleasure that you are experiencing at this moment. Let it wash over you like a warm wave, filling your body and mind with intense feelings of ecstasy and satisfaction. Allow yourself to fully indulge in these sensations, knowing that you are safe and in control at all times.

As you continue to embrace your own sensuality and desire, I want you to repeat these affirmations to yourself.I am fully connected with my own erotic potential.
I am worthy of experiencing pleasure and satisfaction.

Secrets of Men

I am in control of my own desires and can explore them safely and responsibly.

Allow these affirmations to sink deep into your subconscious mind, so that you can access them whenever you need to. Take a deep breath in, and slowly exhale. When you're ready, you can open your eyes and return to your day.

Remember that you have unlocked a powerful source of pleasure within yourself, and that you are capable of experiencing sensations beyond your wildest dreams. Trust yourself and your own desires, and know that you have the power to explore them safely and responsibly.

www.ingramcontent.com/pod-product-compliance
Lightning Source LLC
Chambersburg PA
CBHW072056110526
44590CB00018B/3190